D0365441

THE SUPREME COURT

and

FUNDAMENTAL FREEDOMS

CURRENT POLITICAL PROBLEMS

TAYLOR COLE, EDITOR

Civil Liberties

GEORGE W. SPICER, *The Supreme Court and Fundamental Freedoms*

In preparation

EARL LATHAM, *The Three Constitutions*

JOHN H. HALLOWELL, *Man's Search for Freedom*

WALLACE MENDELSON, *Freedom of Expression*

ROBERT S. RANKIN, *Civil Liberties and Martial Law*

The Supreme Court
and
Fundamental Freedoms

GEORGE W. SPICER
University of Virginia

New York
APPLETON-CENTURY-CROFTS, Inc.

PRINTED IN THE UNITED STATES OF AMERICA

E–83522

For

L. R. S.

For

L. H.

Preface

The purpose of this book is to analyze in brief compass the role of the Supreme Court of the United States as guardian of those constitutional liberties which are assumed to be fundamental both to the well-being of the individual and to the effective operation of democratic institutions. It is regarded as an underlying assumption of the American constitutional system that the liberties of speech, press, assembly and religion, and freedom from arbitrary and unjust discrimination by public authority are essential to the realization of these objectives.

Unfortunately, limitations of space have made it necessary to confine the book to the consideration of those civil liberties which are deemed to be peculiarly fundamental to the realization of the ideals and principles of political democracy. Thus procedural rights have been given only incidental consideration, not because they are not considered important but rather because they are considered less important to the purposes of this work than the substantive rights mentioned.

It is hoped that the book will be useful both to the student of American government and constitutional law, and to the interested general reader.

It is a pleasure to register here my indebtedness to two friends and colleagues, Profesor Robert J. Harris, of Vanderbilt University, and Dean F. D. G. Ribble, of the University of Virginia Law School. The former read the entire manuscript, and the latter read Chapters 1, 3, and 4. Both not only made helpful suggestions for improving the manuscript, but also gave generous encouragement that the book was worthy of publication. Neither, of course, is in any way responsible for its shortcomings.

I am also deeply grateful to the Institute for Research in the

Social Sciences, of the University of Virginia, and to the Richmond Area University Center for financial and stenographic assistance in the preparation of this work.

G. W. S.

Charlottesville, Virginia

Contents

1   Introduction

PURPOSE OF STUDY

The purpose of this book is to analyze briefly the role of the Supreme Court of the United States as guardian of such fundamental rights of the individual as speech, press, assembly, religion, and equal protection of the laws.

Although the interests of liberty are peculiarly those of the individual, they may be equally important to the society of which he is a part. These liberties furnish the undergirding of our democratic political society. Without them political democracy could not survive. The freedom of the electoral process, as reflected in a widely based and uncorrupted suffrage upon which democratic government is directly grounded, would be a meaningless and hollow ritual without the freedom of discussion and continuing debate that is made possible by the underlying rights of free speech, free press, and free assembly. These are the indispensable means for disseminating among the people the ideas and information essential for intelligent self-government. Indeed, self-government implies acceptance and maintenance of these freedoms as conditions which enable the people to continue to govern themselves. As Carl Swisher strikingly put it, "no tenable principles of political liberty will permit political liberty to decree its own execution."[1]

Then, of course, there is the broader social interest in the freedom to pursue and discover truth upon which progress in all phases of life depends. Even if it may be argued that there is no obviously sacred right of the individual to speak, write, teach, publish, it can be demonstrated that it is generally helpful to the

[1] *The Growth of Constitutional Power in the United States* (Chicago, University of Chicago Press, 1946), p. 161.

community to hear what men have to say, to read what they write, and to use what they discover. If these objectives are to be realized, ideas and information—good and bad—must have free access to the open market place of thought and communication, and be free to compete there for acceptance. The community that is denied the opportunity for this exchange is denied political democracy; it is also denied progress. This idea was perhaps most strongly expressed by John Stuart Mill, in his famous *Essay on Liberty*, in 1859. Mill said:

. . . the peculiar evil of silencing the expression of an opinion is that it is robbing the human race; posterity as well as the existing generation; those who dissent from the opinion, still more than those who hold it. If the opinion is right, they are deprived of the opportunity of exchanging error for truth: if wrong, they lose what is almost as great a benefit, the clearer perception and livelier impression of truth, produced by its collision with error.

ROLE OF SUPREME COURT IN SAFEGUARDING THE BASES OF DEMOCRATIC GOVERNMENT

In the American constitutional system, as it has developed over the past century and a half, it is the responsibility of the Supreme Court, though not of the Court alone, to safeguard those values which are essential to the existence of constitutional democracy. For greater understanding and appreciation of what follows, it should be recognized at the outset that the Court, in performing this task, inevitably formulates policy, that is, it performs a political function although in a very different way than does the legislature. This began at least as early as John Marshall's opinion in *Marbury* v. *Madison* in 1803, and has continued to this day.

In this historic opinion Marshall enunciated what came to be described as the doctrine of "judicial review." Only in terms of the application of this doctrine can the American brand of constitutional law be meaningfully defined. As Professor Edward S. Corwin cogently puts it:[2]

As employed in this country, Constitutional Law signifies a body of rules resulting from the interpretation by a high Court of a written constitutional instrument in the course of disposing of cases in which

[2] *Constitution of the United States of America: Analysis and Interpretation* (Washington, Government Printing Office, 1953), Introduction, p. ix.

the validity, in relation to the constitutional instrument, of some act of governmental power, state or national, has been challenged. This function . . . involves the power and duty on the part of the Court of pronouncing void any such act which does not square with its own reading of the Constitutional instrument.

The rationale of this judicial power was authoritatively declared by Chief Justice Marshall in the aforementioned opinion. On the much debated question whether it was intended by the framers of the Constitution that the Court should exercise this power, the Constitution itself is silent. Scholars and jurists differ in their interpretation of what the framers intended. It seems to be generally agreed, however, that a number of the most influential members of the Constitutional Convention of 1787 favored such a power, and assumed that the Court would exercise it. Moreover, as Charles P. Curtis, Jr., said of the authors of the Constitution, "What they left unsaid, they left open for *us* to decide."[3]

It would contribute nothing to our present problem to attempt either to defend or to denounce the alleged partisan motives and political implications of the decision that a section of the Judiciary Act of 1789 was unconstitutional and, therefore, null and void. Certainly it would have been easy for the Court to construe the statutory provision as inapplicable to the situation before it. The fact is that it was held invalid by one who has come to be regarded as the greatest of the Chief Justices of the United States, and many of his admirers have considered the holding a master stroke of judicial statecraft.[4] On the other hand, others have regarded the decision as an unwarranted usurpation.

Whatever the merits of the respective arguments as to origin, the doctrine has long since become firmly established as the most distinctive characteristic of the American constitutional system, and in the words of Woodrow Wilson the Court is "the balance wheel of our whole constitutional system."[5] As conservative a jurist on the question of judicial review as Judge Learned Hand remarked that while "it is impossible to have any assurance how

[3] *Lions Under the Throne* (Boston, Houghton Mifflin, 1947), p. 3.
[4] A. J. Beveridge, *Life of John Marshall* (Boston, Houghton Mifflin, 1919), Vol. III, pp. 142–143.
[5] *Constitutional Government in the United States* (New York, Columbia University Press, 1907), p. 142.

the Convention would have voted at the time . . . it was probable, if indeed it was not certain, that without some arbiter whose
decision should be final, the whole system would have col-
lapsed,"[6] and he thinks that the Court is the best arbiter.

The full story of how the Court achieved this distinctive role
cannot be told here. Suffice it to say that its strength and dur-
ability spring from the fact that the American people look to the
Court as the ultimate guardian of their Constitution and the liberties guaranteed therein. Its strength lies in the support of the people, and over the long pull it reflects the public thought and public
conscience. When it functions at its best, it also helps to frame
and guide the public conscience. Indeed, its highest function on
occasion may be to hold back irrational and prejudiced majorities
until they can give more sober consideration to a question. The
independence and prestige of the Court enable it to resist to a
considerable degree the temporary passions and prejudices of the
people.

Finally, then, it may be said that the Court, in the performance
of its function of judicial review, is the arbiter of the federal system in the settlement of conflicts between the states and the national government; that it fixes the boundaries between the constitutional powers of the legislative and executive branches of the
national government in proper cases; and that it is the guardian of
individual liberty against both national and state governments.

The latter function has been its most important since 1937.
Within this period, judicial review of legislative action has been
largely confined to the field of civil liberties. In the judicial settlement of controversies arising here as elsewhere, the specific language of the Constitution offers little guidance. As Chief Justice
Marshall remarked in *McCulloch* v. *Maryland*,[7] the nature of the
Constitution requires that only its great outlines should be marked,
its important objects designated, and the minor ingredients which
compose those objects be deduced from the nature of the objects
themselves.

In the performance of the function of deducing "minor ingredients," the Court necessarily exercises a wide discretion in in-

[6] *Saturday Review*, March 15, 1958, p. 16.
[7] 4 Wheaton 315 (1819).

terpreting and applying such a concept, for example, as due process of law. The interpretation of what the Constitution commands here has been of a changing nature, as the Court majority has developed this concept in the face of changing conditions and varying climates of opinion. First, due process was only a procedural safeguard; it simply guaranteed a fair trial. Near the end of the last century it was given a substantive content and was applied by the Court to protect property rights but not personal rights, at least not for another quarter of a century. Then, in 1925, the due process clause of the Fourteenth Amendment became the principal constitutional safeguard of individual freedom.

Thus, it is important to recognize that judges deciding civil liberties cases in such a constitutional context may choose from among many legally applicable formulas and techniques and that the choices made necessarily result in policy decisions. In such a situation the rules made by judges necessarily reflect their views, and they reflect, as Judge Jerome Frank has pointed out, "judicial compromises or adjustment between conflicting social interests, and thus express judgments of value or policy."[8]

Back of the intricate array of formulas that are applied with varying degrees of emphasis in the cases lies a common problem of judicial interpretation which runs through all civil liberties controversies, namely, a conflict of interests, and the Court must of necessity make a choice between the values involved in this conflict. When, for example, the Court declared invalid a series of handbill ordinances forbidding the distribution of handbills on the streets, it was expressing the value judgment that free speech is more important to the community than the object of maintaining clean streets by this method.

As already indicated, none of this is to suggest that courts make policy in the same way as does the legislature. The legislature formally initiates policy, whereas the courts can only act retrospectively in specific cases involving bona fide antagonists. The content of legislative policy may be ascertained merely by an examination of the statutes, but judicial policy grows out of rulings in specific controversies and its content can, as a rule, be deter-

[8] *Courts on Trial: Myths and Reality in American Justice* (Princeton, Princeton University Press, 1949), p. 265.

mined only by a review of the totality of cases dealing with a given subject. Even then, the results are sometimes obscure and confusing.

Finally, it should be noted, the Court does not bear sole responsibility for the protection of individual liberties. The Congress, the state legislatures, the President and governors, and the citizens all share in this responsibility. Yet, though the courts cannot do everything in this connection, they can and have done much. Moreover, as already indicated, the judges have, since at least the early 1920's, been our principal teachers in civil liberties. Their statements in explanation of their decisions are not infrequently more important than the decisions themselves. The eloquent statements of such justices as Holmes, Brandeis, Hughes, Black, Frankfurter, and others have been profoundly influential in developing a popular appreciation of constitutional liberties.

SCOPE OF STUDY

Only those civil liberties which are deemed to be peculiarly fundamental to the foregoing ideals and principles are examined in this study. Procedural rights are not discussed except where they may be incidental to the consideration of substantive rights. This is not to suggest that procedural rights are not of great importance. Limitations of space alone have compelled their exclusion.

In subsequent chapters, attention will be given to the following matters: (1) the Court's development of civil liberties doctrine before 1937, (2) the Court's role in the expansion of the constitutional law of freedom of speech, press, and assembly in the decade after 1937, (3) the extension of protection of religious freedom under the First and Fourteenth Amendments and the Court's struggle with the constitutional prohibition of the establishment of religion, (4) the Court's response to problems of social and political equality involved in racial discrimination, (5) the Court's response to the problems of civil liberty and national security presented by the "cold war," and (6) a summary of the Court's achievements and some continuing threats to civil liberties.

The high points in the Court's development of civil liberties principles before 1937 (the beginning of the period emphasized in this book), which are of major importance to subsequent expansion of civil liberties, are: (1) the judicial interpretation by which First Amendment freedoms were incorporated into the "liberty" of the due process clause of the Fourteenth Amendment, and thus made applicable to state action and subject to the supervision of the federal courts; (2) the enunciation of the "clear and present danger" test by Justice Holmes in the Schenck case[9] in 1919, and its refinement and expansion by Justice Brandeis with Holmes' support in the Whitney case[10] in 1927; (3) the formulation of the "bad tendency" test as a gloss upon the older "reasonable man" test in the Gitlow case[11] in 1925.

Much the most significant of these developments was the first. Judicial high points in this development include the declaration of the Court in the Gitlow case that First Amendment freedoms are among the fundamental personal liberties "protected by due process clause of the Fourteenth Amendment from impairment by the States," and the case of *Near* v. *Minnesota*[12] which was the first case to hold invalid (in 1931) a state act because it violated First Amendment freedoms in its substantive provisions. These doctrines will be further analyzed and explained in Chapter 2.

Chapter 3 will emphasize the application of the clear and present danger test to a series of new and different situations in the decade after 1937—situations involving mainly the collision of First Amendment freedoms with the exercise of the police power of the state in fields of general welfare not closely related to the necessities of national security. It was in this area that the Court clarified and reinforced the clear and present danger test by the theory of "preferred status" of First Amendment freedoms. Under this theory, which will be critically discussed in Chapter 2, the Court majority raised the constitutional barriers against governmental regulations of speech, press, assembly, and religion. It

[9] *Schenck* v. *United States,* 249 U.S. 47 (1919).
[10] *Whitney* v. *California,* 274 U.S. 357 (1927).
[11] *Gitlow* v. *New York,* 268 U.S. 652 (1925).
[12] 283 U.S. 697 (1931).

placed the burden of proof on the government to establish the validity of an act, appearing on its face to restrict any of these freedoms, by showing that the exercise of the freedom created a clear and present danger of a substantive evil within the power of the legislature to forbid.

As thus reinforced, the clear and present danger test was applied to extend the protection of freedom of expression to such new situations as picketing, criticism of judicial conduct, the distribution of handbills, and speech in public places through sound trucks, and motion pictures. An examination of the cases will demonstrate that in these areas the Court tended to give maximum scope to freedom by holding restraint to the minimum imposed by clear and present danger. In some cases involving these questions, the Court so applied the clear and present danger doctrine as to suggest an absolutist concept of First Amendment freedoms.

Such a conception was, for example, expressed by Justice Black in *Bridges* v. *California* in these words:[13]

What finally emerges from the "clear and present danger" cases is a working principle that the substantive evils must be extremely serious and the degree of imminence extremely high before the utterance can be punished. These cases do not purport to mark the furthermost constitutional boundaries of protected expression, nor do we here. They do no more than recognize a minimum compulsion of the Bill of Rights. For the First Amendment does not speak equivocally. It prohibits any law abridging the freedom of speech or of the press. It must be taken as a command of the broadest scope that explicit language, read in the context of a liberty-loving society will allow.

Although the clear and present danger test has been substantially modified by the Court in "cold war" cases, to be considered later, it appears to have continued validity in the areas of freedom of expression (such as those examined in Chapter 3) which conflict with the public welfare of the community, as distinguished from freedom of expression which conflicts with national security. In the latter situation, the Court has the far more difficult problem of determining how far a free society must extend its freedom to those who are dedicated to the destruction of that society by force.

13 314 U.S. 252, 263 (1941).

2   Historical Background

The Constitution as originally adopted contained no restriction upon freedom of expression and of religion except the prohibition of any religious qualification for holding office and a provision freeing the members of the House and the Senate from any responsibility for their utterances in their respective Chambers except to the members thereof. Even though the First Amendment became a part of the fundamental law in 1791, it is interesting to note that the judicial development of the constitutional law of free speech and free press, as guaranteed by this amendment, did not begin until the end of World War I, and the course of development with respect to religious freedom was not substantially different. The explanation for this situation lies in the dual fact that the First Amendment, like other provisions of the federal Bill of Rights, was directed only at the national government, not at the states, and that Congress, with the one glaring exception of the Alien and Sedition Acts of 1798, avoided encroachment upon these liberties for more than a century and a quarter. Moreover, this legislation, which was never tested by the Supreme Court, was effectively repudiated in the election of 1800. Except, then, for the Executive suppression of criticism of governmental policies during the Civil War, the national government took no action raising freedom of expression issues until passage of the Espionage Act of 1917.

With our entrance into World War I, Congress, spurred on by the stimulus of popular hysteria, enacted the Espionage Act of 1917, imposing restrictions on speech for the first time since 1798. This time the Supreme Court was quickly drawn into the controversy and thus entered upon its uneven course in the development of freedom of communication doctrine.

EXPANDING SCOPE OF FIRST AMENDMENT FREEDOMS

First Amendment freedoms, more particularly freedom of speech and press, have through recent judicial interpretation come to mean much more than was indicated for many years after the adoption of the amendment. For some time after the amendment's adoption, freedom of speech and press was interpreted by commentators and state courts to mean only freedom from previous *restraint* in the Blackstonian sense. Blackstone was, of course, stating a rule of the English Constitution as it was understood in 1769 when he wrote that "The liberty of the press is indeed essential to the nature of a free state; but this consists in laying no previous restraints upon publications, and not in freedom from censure for criminal matter when published," and if one "publishes what is improper, mischievous, or illegal, he must take the consequences of his own temerity."[1] To Blackstone this was the whole of freedom of expression. By the terms of this test, the government may impose no restraint before the words are spoken or printed but may punish after utterance or publication at its discretion.

Even Justice Holmes went so far, in 1907, as to declare that the First Amendment had enacted Blackstone's definition of freedom of expression. Said he in *Patterson* v. *Colorado:*[2]

> The main purpose of such constitutional provisions is to prevent all such previous restraints upon publications as had been practiced by other governments, and they do not prevent the subsequent punishment of such as may be deemed contrary to the public welfare. The preliminary freedom extends to the false as well as to the true; the subsequent punishment may extend to the true as to the false.

It is, of course, well known that Justice Holmes later repudiated this view.

In 1931, Chief Justice Hughes, in *Near* v. *Minnesota,*[3] the first great free press case decided by the Supreme Court, modified both sides of the Blackstonian formula. Admitting that immunity from

---

[1] *Commentaries,* Vol. IV, p. 151.
[2] 205 U.S. 454 (1907).
[3] 283 U.S. 697 (1931).

previous restraint is deserving of special emphasis, that immunity, he declared, "cannot be deemed to exhaust the conception of the liberty guaranteed by the state and federal constitutions." Freedom to punish for publication could render liberty of the press "a mockery and a delusion." Thus, "It is now clear that if subsequent penalties may constitute abridgments under the First Amendment, it is also true that some forms of prior restraint may be perfectly proper." Although "prior restraint" has experienced a considerable diversity of interpretation and application in subsequent cases, the general tendency, especially in the more recent cases, has been to evaluate its operation in the light of particular circumstances confronting the Court.[4]

"ABSORPTION" OF FIRST AMENDMENT FREEDOMS INTO FOURTEENTH AMENDMENT

Although this study is primarily concerned with the period from 1937 to the present, the judicial developments of this period cannot be understood without some knowledge of earlier developments. Prior to 1937, the Supreme Court had made important advances in the area of civil liberties which prepared the way for the development of the constitutional law of civil liberty from that date on. Unquestionably the most significant of these advances was the judicial interpretation by which the First Amendment freedoms were included in the liberty of the due process of law clause of the Fourteenth Amendment, thus rendering state action in this realm subject to the supervision of the federal courts.

But for its application to the states through the Fourteenth Amendment, the First Amendment would be of relatively little significance. It has already been noted that no case involving federal restriction of freedom of expression reached the Supreme Court until the end of World War I. At this time there was a rapid flurry of cases growing out of the enactment by Congress of the Espionage Act of 1917 and the Sedition Act of 1918. Although some of these cases led to the enunciation of important free speech doctrines (to be considered later

[4] See *Niemotko* v. *Maryland,* 340 U.S. 268; *Kunz* v. *New York,* 340 U.S. 290; *Feiner* v. *New York,* 340 U.S. 315.

under the appropriate heading), no serious questions concerning the constitutionality of the statutes were raised. After this series of cases ended, no further cases involving federal restrictions of First Amendment rights reached the Court until World War II.

In the meantime, however, the Supreme Court's expansion of the due process clause of the Fourteenth Amendment to include the freedoms of the First Amendment had brought to the Court a constant stream of cases involving state restrictions of First Amendment freedoms. Thus, the First Amendment through the Fourteenth has become the focal point of judicial review.

The evolution of this doctrine, whereby the enforcement of First Amendment freedoms against the states was made effective through the Fourteenth Amendment, is one of the most interesting and important aspects of American constitutional jurisprudence. Although it seems reasonably clear that such application was the intention of the framers of the Fourteenth Amendment, the Supreme Court thwarted this development for more than a half century. In the famous Slaughter House cases of 1873, the Court so narrowed the scope of the privileges and immunities clause as to render it virtually meaningless and scornfully rejected the argument that due process possessed a substantive meaning.

The Supreme Court rigidly adhered to this interpretation of the Fourteenth Amendment until the end of the nineteenth century. By judicial interpretation, the due process clause was given a substantive content in the late 1890's. Under this interpretation the substance or content of a state law must be reasonable in order to be constitutional. But the doctrine was first applied to safeguard property rights and the liberty of contract,[5] chiefly of corporations, from state police power in the form of social legislation, and was destined to be rejected as the basis for the protection of civil liberties against state encroachment for another quarter century. This is ironical when it is remembered that the primary purpose of the Fourteenth Amendment was to safeguard the personal and

[5] See *Smyth* v. *Ames,* 169 U.S. 466 (1898); *Holden* v. *Hardy,* 169 U.S. 366 (1898); *Lochner* v. *New York,* 198 U.S. 45 (1905).

civil rights of the Negroes who had been freed from slavery by the Thirteenth Amendment.

Indeed, as late as 1922, in *Prudential Life Insurance Co.* v. *Cheek*,[6] the Supreme Court bluntly asserted that "neither the Fourteenth Amendment nor any other provision of the Constitution imposes any restrictions upon the state about freedom of speech." It is clear then that for a quarter of a century the Court had readily accepted freedom of contract as a constitutionally guaranteed liberty but had steadfastly refused to give an equal status to freedom of speech, press, assembly, and religion. Clearly the Court could not persist in this illogical and indefensible position. Some indication of what was to come was indicated in certain dissenting opinions. As early as 1907, Justice Harlan had concluded: "It is, I think, impossible to conceive of liberty as secured by the constitution against hostile action, whether by the nation or by the states, which does not embrace the right to enjoy free speech and the right to have a free press."[7] More pointedly, Mr. Justice Brandeis remarked in *Gilbert* v. *Minnesota*,[8] in 1920: "I cannot believe that the liberty guaranteed by the Fourteenth Amendment includes only liberty to acquire and to enjoy property." In this case even the majority had assumed for the sake of argument that freedom of speech, guaranteed in the First Amendment, restricted state action, but it was found that if such a right did exist it had not been violated in the case before the Court.

Three years later, and only one year after the outspoken declaration to the contrary in the Cheek case, the Court gave a clear indication that it was abandoning its reluctance to intervene in the encroachments of state governments upon fundamental personal freedoms. In *Meyer* v. *Nebraska*[9] in 1923, the Court held invalid a state law forbidding German language instruction because the due process clause of the Fourteenth Amendment protected both the right of the teacher to pursue his calling and the right of the parents to control the education of their children. Despite the

---

[6] 259 U.S. 530 (1922).
[7] *Patterson* v. *Colorado*, 205 U.S. 454 (1907).
[8] 254 U.S. 325, 343 (1920).
[9] 262 U.S. 390 (1923).

continued emphasis upon property rights, the Court's definition of the "liberty" protected by the Fourteenth Amendment went much further. Said Justice McReynolds for the Court:

Without doubt, it denotes not merely freedom from bodily restraint, but also the right of the individual to contract, to engage in any of the common occupations of life, to acquire useful knowledge, to marry, establish a home and bring up children, to worship God according to the dictates of his own conscience, and generally, to enjoy those privileges long recognized at common law as essential to the orderly pursuit of happiness by free men.

Then, in 1925, the great reversal became complete and unmistakable in an almost casual manner. In *Gitlow* v. *New York*,[10] the Court, sustaining New York's "criminal anarchy" law against the claim of a New York Communist that it deprived him of freedom of speech and press in contravention of the due process of law clause of the Fourteenth Amendment, made this significant proposition: "For present purposes we may and do assume that freedom of speech and of the press—which are protected by the First Amendment from abridgment by Congress—are among the fundamental personal rights and 'liberties' protected by the due process clause of the Fourteenth Amendment from impairment by the states."

The assumption here made found expression in explicit decisions over the next several years. Two years later, in *Fiske* v. *Kansas*,[11] a statute similar to that involved in the Gitlow case was held invalid as applied because it violated the due process clause of the Fourteenth Amendment. This Kansas statute which, among other things, provided for the punishment of any person who "advocates . . . or teaches the duty, necessity, propriety or expediency of crime, criminal syndicalism or sabotage" was applied by the state court as covering a case involving only membership in, and the securing of other members for, an organization whose constitution proclaimed the incompatibility of interests and the inevitability of the struggle between employers and workers until the ultimate triumph of the latter. The statute as thus applied was held by the Supreme Court to deprive the defendant of liberty

10 268 U.S. 652 (1925).
11 274 U.S. 380 (1927).

without due process of law. The first state act to be held invalid because it violated First Amendment freedoms in its substantive provisions was the Minnesota "gag-press law," which provided for the padlocking by injunctive process of newspapers publishing "scandalous, malicious, defamatory or obscene" material. In holding this statute to be an unwarranted previous restraint on freedom of the press, Chief Justice Hughes declared for the Court in 1931: [12] "It is no longer open to doubt that the liberty of the press and of speech is within the liberty safeguarded from invasion by state action." In subsequent cases the Court has added freedom of assembly,[13] freedom of religion,[14] and establishment of religion [15] to the liberty guaranteed against state restraint.

It is, of course, clear that not all civil liberties of the federal Bill of Rights have been read into the term *liberty* in the Fourteenth Amendment. Only those liberties which the Court regards as basic or fundamental have been absorbed into the due process clause of the Fourteenth Amendment. These include freedom of religion, freedom of speech, freedom of the press, and freedom of assembly and petition. Mr. Justice Cardozo, in a case decided in 1937, referred to these rights as essential to "a scheme of ordered liberty." They are regarded as so vital to the preservation of our democratic system that they stand upon "a different plane of social and moral values." For illustration, Mr. Cardozo said of freedom of thought and speech "that it is the matrix, the indispensable condition, of nearly every other form of freedom." [16]

Many of the guarantees of the federal Bill of Rights, however, have been held not to be of such vital importance as "to be implicit in the concept of ordered liberty," and thus are not protected against state action by the Fourteenth Amendment. From 1884 on, the Supreme Court had rejected the contention that certain procedural guarantees of the federal Bill of Rights were binding upon the states. Nothing in the Fourteenth Amendment compelled a state to afford a person accused of crime a grand jury indict-

[12] *Near* v. *Minnesota*, 283 U.S. 697 (1931); see also *Grosjean* v. *American Press Co.*, 297 U.S. 233 (1936).
[13] *De Jonge* v. *Oregon*, 299 U.S. 353 (1937).
[14] *Cantwell* v. *Connecticut*, 310 U.S. 296 (1940).
[15] *Everson* v. *Board of Education*, 330 U.S. (1947).
[16] *Palko* v. *Connecticut*, 302 U.S. 319 (1937).

ment,[17] or a jury trial,[18] or immunity from self-incrimination,[19] or freedom from double jeopardy.[20] Although these procedural rights are important, admitted Justice Cardozo in the Palko case, "they are not the very essence of a scheme of ordered liberty. To abolish them is not to violate a 'principle of justice so rooted in the traditions and conscience of our people as to be ranked as fundamental.' . . . Few would be so narrow or provincial as to maintain that a fair and enlightened system of justice would be impossible without them."

JUDICIAL TESTS DEVISED BY THE COURT

Although the guarantees of the First Amendment are expressed in the most sweeping and unequivocal terms, they have never been regarded as absolute, but are subject to restrictions for the protection of the public safety and welfare. Hence the Court has found it necessary to devise tests or standards and to create presumptions to guide it in striking the proper balance between the public interest and the private right alleged to be invaded in a given case.

This the Court has not found an easy task. In cases involving these freedoms, the Court's task of interpretation differs from that in many other cases. Here it is faced not merely with a question of whether a power has been granted to the national government or reserved to the states, in which case there is the presumption of constitutionality, but in cases involving freedom of speech and press, or of religion, the Court must interpret and apply a power granted to Congress, or more often one reserved to the states, and at the same time interpret and apply a constitutional limitation on governmental power. Power, of course, is essential to and inherent in government. Yet it is an essential of the American system of constitutional democracy that governmental power be limited. To make this principle doubly sure, the Bill of Rights and other amendments were added to the Constitution. Moreover, the difficulty of the Court's task has been increased by virtue of the

[17] *Hurtado* v. *California*, 110 U.S. 516 (1884).
[18] *Maxwell* v. *Dow*, 176 U.S. 581 (1900).
[19] *Twining* v. *New Jersey*, 211 U.S. 78 (1908).
[20] *Palko* v. *Connecticut*, 302 U.S. 319 (1937).

fact that First Amendment freedoms, as indicated previously, have been regarded by the Court as peculiarly fundamental in a democratic society. Here, as will later be shown, the usual course of presumption of constitutionality is not so readily available.

Thus there was need for principles of judicial construction, and the Supreme Court, spurred on first by World War I espionage and sedition legislation and later by the new doctrine of "nationalization" enunciated in the Gitlow case, set about to establish them.

By 1925, the Court had formulated several such tests: (1) the "clear and present danger" test, (2) the "bad tendency" test, and (3) later, a supplement to clear and present danger known as "preferred status" of First Amendment freedoms. Interrelated with (1) and (2) is the test of "evil intent." Only the briefest consideration of these tests can be undertaken here.

Clear and Present Danger Test

In the first Supreme Court free speech case of *Schenck* v. *United States*,[21] decided shortly after the First World War, Mr. Justice Holmes sought to set forth a standard for the Court in terms of the now famous clear and present danger doctrine. He said:

The question in every case is whether the words are used in such circumstances and are of such a nature as to create a clear and present danger that they will bring about the substantive evils that Congress has a right to prevent. It is a question of proximity and degree. When a nation is at war many things that might be said in time of peace are such a hindrance to its effort that their utterance will not be endured so long as men fight, and that no court could regard them as protected by any constitutional right.

In this case a clear and present danger was found to exist, and the doctrine was applied to sustain the application of the Espionage Act of 1917 to Schenck's distribution of antidraft leaflets to men who were subject to military service, urging them in intemperate and impassioned language to resist the draft.

The second case in which the clear and present danger test was at issue was *Abrams* v. *United States*,[22] in which the Court

[21] 249 U.S. 47 (1919).   [22] 250 U.S. 616 (1919).

sustained the application of the Sedition Act of 1918 to the distribution of Marxist pamphlets urging the workers of the world to resist the Allied and American intervention against the Bolsheviki after the Russian revolution. Holmes, with the concurrence of Brandeis, dissented, insisting that no threat of clear and present danger to our safety had been shown. On this occasion Holmes states his theory much more sharply in these words: "I think that we should be eternally vigilant against attempts to check the expression of opinions that we loathe and believe to be fraught with death, unless they so imminently threaten immediate interference with the lawful and pressing purposes of the law that an immediate check is required to save the country."

It should be noted that in none of the cases decided before 1927 did Justices Holmes and Brandeis use the clear and present danger test for the purpose of challenging the constitutional validity of a federal or state statute. The constitutionality of the Sedition Act of 1918 was not questioned, nor was that of state statutes of a similar nature. It would seem clear, then, that Holmes' Schenck formula was meant only as a "rule of reason" to guide administrative authorities and the courts in the application of the act, and not as a test of the power of Congress to enact substantive legislation. In the application of the law, Holmes and Brandeis sought to give freedom of expression the maximum scope by requiring the showing of a clear and present danger.

In 1927, however, in *Whitney* v. *California*[23] Justice Brandeis, with the support of Holmes, set forth the doctrine as the basis on which the power of the legislative body to limit freedom of expression could be challenged by evidence that there was no emergency sufficiently grave and imminent to warrant it. Here Brandeis asserted that a legislative declaration of the existence of a danger sufficiently serious to justify restrictions on speech and assembly did no more than create a "rebuttable presumption." If the Court found that the conditions alleged by the legislature did not exist, it should refuse to enforce the law on the ground that no clear and present danger existed. In other words, in a case where the validity of a statute is dependent upon the existence of

[23] 274 U.S. 357 (1927).

certain conditions, the enactment of the statute will not, alone, establish the facts essential to its validity.

In this case Justice Brandeis, in a concurring opinion in which Holmes joined, restated and refined the clear and present danger doctrine in a masterly civil liberties statement. Although both voted with the majority to sustain the conviction of the defendant under the California Criminal Syndicalism Act, on the basis of evidence that tended to establish the existence of a conspiracy to commit serious crimes, they disagreed with the majority on the validity of a section of the act which not only made it a felony punishable by imprisonment to advocate or teach, or practice criminal syndicalism (the overthrow of the government by violence), but was also aimed "at association with those who proposed to preach it."

In his restatement of the theory, Brandeis in part declared:

> Fear of serious injury cannot alone justify suppression of free speech and assembly. . . . There must be reasonable ground to fear that serious evil will result if free speech is practiced. There must be reasonable ground to believe that the danger apprehended is imminent. There must be reasonable ground to believe that the evil to be prevented is a serious one. . . . In order to support a finding of clear and present danger it must be shown either that immediate serious violence was to be expected or was advocated, or that the past conduct furnished reason to believe that advocacy was then contemplated. . . . No danger flowing from speech can be deemed clear and present, unless the incidence of the evil apprehended is so imminent that it may befall before there is opportunity for full discussion. . . .

Although Holmes and Brandeis were never again to speak of the clear and present danger test, and although for ten years after Whitney the Supreme Court made no specific reference to the test, the Whitney formula nevertheless set the pattern which the majority of the Court followed when it finally accepted and applied the doctrine for the first time in 1937 to protect the libertarian claims of the defendant in the case of *Herndon* v. *Lowry*.[24]

In the meantime a number of cases vigorously sustaining libertarian claims were decided without reference to clear and present danger. Moreover, these cases were of pioneer significance

24 301 U.S. 242 (1937).

in the development of freedom of expression and freedom of assembly with respect to state encroachment. Three cases involved direct application of the tremendously important principle, first enunciated by the majority of the Court in the dictum of the Gitlow case, that the fundamental rights of the First Amendment are embodied in the concept of liberty guaranteed against state encroachment by the Fourteenth Amendment.[25]

The failure of the Supreme Court to recognize the clear and present danger test even by name for a decade raised doubt as to whether it was any longer valid as a component of judicial decision. Then, in the constitutionally significant year of 1937, the Court for the first time applied the doctrine to invalidate a statute limiting freedom of expression. Thus it will be seen that for the first eighteen years of its history the doctrine never enjoyed full acceptance by the Supreme Court, but in the period from 1937 to about 1946 the stone which had been rejected became the head of the corner, and was applied by the Court in a variety of situations, which will be considered subsequently. But the doctrine never gained the approval of all the justices. Justice Frankfurter has been its most vigorous and consistent antagonist.

Bad Tendency Test

The bad tendency test which was applied by the Court in the Gitlow case, and by the majority of the Court in the Whitney case, was essentially antithetical to clear and present danger and consequently much less favorable to freedom of expression.

In *Gitlow* v. *New York*, the majority of the Court rejected Mr. Justice Holmes' clear and present danger test and sustained the application of the New York Criminal Anarchy Statute of 1902 to the publication by a Left-wing Socialist of a manifesto in which it was claimed that humanity could be saved from capitalism "only by the Communist Revolution." It was not claimed that the publication posed any immediate threat to the safety of New York state, but the majority ruled that even though publications and speeches themselves create no immediate danger, they may be punished by the legislature if they have a "tendency" to bring

---

[25] *Near* v. *Minnesota,* 283 U.S. 697 (1931); *Grosjean* v. *American Press Co.,* 297 U.S. 233 (1936); *De Jonge* v. *Oregon,* 299 U.S. 353 (1937).

about results dangerous to public safety. Mr. Justice Sanford declared for the Court majority that it was "not open to question" that a state could punish utterances "tending to corrupt public morals, incite to crime, or disturb the public peace. . . ." It was enough "if the natural tendency and probable effect was to bring about the substantive evils which the legislative body might prevent."[26] Furthermore, "Every presumption is to be indulged in favor of the validity of the statute." Legislative conclusions are to be declared invalid only if they are clearly arbitrary and unreasonable.

The bad tendency test is, then, nothing more than a gloss upon an earlier standard of judicial review known as the "reasonable man" test. By this standard the Court must not strike down a legislative judgment expressed in a statute if a fair and "reasonable man" could have reached the same conclusion as the legislature. Before the Whitney case it was possible to reconcile this theory with clear and present danger by arguing that they were applicable to different circumstances. For example, Justice Sanford argued in Gitlow that the clear and present danger test had no application "where the legislative body itself has previously determined the danger of substantive evil arising from utterances of a specified character."

But after Brandeis and Holmes had restated clear and present danger in Whitney as a basis on which the constitutionality of a law abridging free speech and assembly could be challenged by evidence that there was no emergency justifying it, there was no way of reconciling clear and present danger and the reasonable man theory except by giving a preferential status to First Amendment freedoms.

Preferred Status Doctrine

It is interesting that Justice Holmes, who evolved the clear and present danger test, was also an ardent champion of the reasonable man test in cases involving economic regulation. In his famous dissent to *Lochner* v. *New York*,[27] he declared that he would not hold invalid a statute "unless it can be said that a rational and

---

[26] 268 U.S. 652, 671 (1925).
[27] 198 U.S. 45 (1905).

fair man necessarily would admit that the statute proposed would infringe fundamental principles as they have been understood by the traditions of our people and our law." Yet there is implicit in the application of clear and present danger to First Amendment freedoms alone a preference for a more liberal scope for these than for other constitutional rights.

Holmes never gave an explicit and satisfactory explanation of why legislation limiting First Amendment rights must pass the clear and present danger test, whereas other legislation must simply pass the test of reasonableness.[28] It remained for other justices later to provide the rationale for the Holmes doctrine. On the face of this, it could plausibly be argued that Justice Holmes was inconsistent. A more reasonable explanation, however, for the apparent paradox is that Holmes believed that his judicial function called for a more exacting standard of judicial review in cases dealing with First Amendment freedoms than in those concerning procedural rights and economic matters. Certainly a strong case can be made for this position.

If First Amendment freedoms are fundamental in the sense that Justice Cardozo argued in the Palko case, that is, in the sense that they are the bases of nearly all other freedoms, it would seem only logical for the Court to apply more exacting standards of review in cases dealing with those liberties than in economic cases. Furthermore, as Justice Stone indicated in his now famous footnote to *United States* v. *Carolene Products Co.*[29] in 1938, it would seem elementary to the principles of constitutional democracy that "legislation which restricts those political processes" by which undesirable legislation may be repealed should "be subjected to more exacting judicial scrutiny under the general prohibitions of the Fourteenth Amendment than are most other types of legislation." If, for example, a popular majority of today should impose controls on certain economic activities, another popular majority of tomorrow with a different view may remove such controls, so long as the political processes by which such changes are effected remain free and unobstructed. This is not so

---

[28] See C. H. Pritchett, *Civil Liberties and the Vinson Court* (Chicago, University of Chicago Press, 1954), pp. 28ff.
[29] 304 U.S. 144 (1938).

with legislation limiting freedom of expression and assembly. If the majority of the moment suppresses those with whom they disagree, the minority is precluded even from arguing that a wrong has been done and that improvements are possible. Obstruction of the democratic process is not self-corrective. There is reason, then, for a court to intervene to insure freedom of discussion of possible changes and improvements in the affairs of the people and not to intervene in behalf of one economic theory rather than another.

Justice Stone also suggested that similar considerations might enter into the review of statutes directed at religious, national, or racial minorities, that "prejudice against discrete and insular minorities may be a special condition which tends seriously to curtail the operation of those political processes ordinarily to be relied upon to protect minorities, and which may call for a correspondingly more searching judicial inquiry."

The idea thus backhandedly suggested by Justice Stone in 1938, and clearly implied by Justice Cardozo in 1937, had by 1939, in the first handbill cases, become the doctrine of a clear majority of the Court. Of legislative abridgment of the rights of free speech and press, Justice Roberts said in these cases: "Mere legislative preferences or beliefs respecting matters of public convenience may well support regulation directed at other personal activities, but be insufficient to justify such as diminishes the exercise of rights so vital to the maintenance of democratic institutions."

As further developed in other cases in the 1940's, the preferred status doctrine became the supplement to, and the rationale of, the clear and present danger test. The relationship of the two concepts is well illustrated by this statement of Justice Jackson in the second flag salute case:[30]

The right of a state to regulate, for example, a public utility may well include, so far as the due process test is concerned, power to impose all of the restrictions which a legislature may have a "rational basis" for adopting. But freedoms of speech and press, of assembly, and of worship may not be infringed on such slender grounds. They are

[30] *West Virginia State Board of Education* v. *Barnette,* 319 U.S. 624 (1943).

susceptible of restriction only to prevent grave and immediate danger to interests which the state may lawfully protect.

In the language of the cases, the doctrine of clear and present danger as reinforced by preferred status may be briefly stated as follows: The liberties protected by the First Amendment, and made applicable to the states through the Fourteenth Amendment, are so peculiarly important to the maintenance of democratic institutions that they enjoy a preferred status in our scale of constitutional values, and thus any legislative act which appears on its face to restrict any of those liberties is presumed to be unconstitutional, and the burden of proof is on those who defend such legislation to show that it is justified by clear and present danger to the public interest.[31]

The Test of Evil Intent

The state of the speaker's mind has usually been an important factor in the determination of the danger of speech. Sometimes coupled with, and sometimes distinct from, the bad tendency and clear and present danger tests, the Court has applied the test of evil intent. The cases give little clue as to how obvious the evil intent must be before it can be of constitutional significance, but the Court is apparently more likely to sustain the punishment of speech if the speaker clearly meant to bring about the substantive evil. Only a few examples of the application of this concept of evil intent can be given here.

In the Gitlow case, words having an evil tendency and uttered with evil intent were held to be punishable. In the previously mentioned case of *Fiske* v. *Kansas,* the Court reversed the conviction of an I.W.W. organizer under the Kansas antisyndicalism law on the ground that there was no evidence that the defendant intended to effect his industrial and political ends by violence or other unlawful means. Here it was not suggested that there was no clear and present danger that such an intent would have resulted in illegal action. Yet, in *Whitney* v. *California,* Justice Brandeis restated the clear and present danger test to include the intent to create such danger. Still a different combination of intent with

---

[31] See Robert E. Cushman, "Civil Liberties," *American Political Science Review,* Vol. 42 (February, 1948), pp. 42–43.

other elements was illustrated in the Yates case, where the Court held that advocacy of violent overthrow of the government, even with intent to bring about violent overthrow, could not be punished under the Smith Act unless the language employed was calculated to incite to action.[32]

[32] See Chapter 7.

FREEDOM OF SPEECH AND PRESS:
CLEAR AND PRESENT DANGER TEST

As was pointed out in Chapter 2, the Supreme Court, for the first time, in 1937, in the Herndon case applied the clear and present danger test to uphold the civil liberties claims of the defendant.[1] Here, the Court was faced with the conflicting claims of the clear and present danger test and the bad tendency test which the Court had applied in the Gitlow case. The Court set aside the conviction of Herndon under a Georgia anti-insurrection law for attempting to incite insurrection. The evidence on which Herndon was convicted in the state court consisted of his admission that he had held meetings for the purpose of recruiting membership for the Communist Party, and certain printed matter found in a box which he carried when arrested. In upholding the conviction the Georgia courts applied the tests of *evil intent* of the speaker and *evil tendency* of his words. The Supreme Court, however, found the act as applied bad because "The legislature of Georgia has not made membership in the Communist party unlawful by reason of its supposed dangerous tendency," and judge and jury had not found that the defendant's utterances constituted "a clear and present danger of forcible obstruction of a particular state function."

Mr. Justice Roberts, speaking for the majority of five, further declared:

The power of a state to abridge freedom of speech and assembly is the exception rather than the rule and the penalizing even of utterances of a defined character must find its justification in a reasonable apprehension of danger to organized government. The judgment of the legisla-

[1] *Herndon* v. *Lowry,* 301 U.S. 242 (1937).

ture is not unfettered. The limitation upon individual liberty must have appropriate relation to the safety of the state. Legislation which goes beyond this need violates the principle of the Constitution.

Thus for the first time a majority of the Court accepted and applied the doctrine of clear and present danger and embarked upon a course which, during the following decade, led to the acceptance of a near absolutist conception of First Amendment freedoms. In these years the doctrine was amplified and applied in a variety of new and unusual situations. This is not to suggest that clear and present danger was the sole test of free speech restriction. It was merely the principal one and the one most consistently employed for libertarian results. Nor did its employment always embody the same judgment factors. Rather, it embodied a variety of factors given greater or lesser weight according to the circumstances of each case.

Picketing as Freedom of Expression

One of the most interesting examples of judicial expression of the concept of freedom of speech is the inclusion of picketing within its protection as a means of persuasion and communication in labor disputes. The first indication that the Court would regard picketing as a form of free speech protected by the Fourteenth Amendment occurred in 1937 in *Senn* v. *Tile Layers Protective Union*,[2] which sustained the constitutionality of a Wisconsin statute legalizing peaceful picketing.

Three years later, in *Thornhill* v. *Alabama*[3] and *Carlson* v. *California*[4] decided on the same day, the intimation of the *Senn* case that picketing is a form of free speech was confirmed. Applying the doctrine of clear and present danger, the Supreme Court invalidated statutes of Alabama and California against peaceful picketing, including the carrying of signs and banners. In the Thornhill case the Court held unconstitutional an Alabama statute forbidding peaceful picketing. Freedom of speech and press guaranteed by the Constitution includes "at least the liberty to discuss publicly and truthfully all matters of public concern with-

[2] 301 U.S. 468 (1937).
[3] 310 U.S. 98 (1940).
[4] 310 U.S. 106 (1940).

out previous restraint or fear of subsequent punishment." Hence
the Court concluded that, "In the circumstances of our times the
dissemination of information concerning the facts of a labor dispute must be regarded as within the area of free discussion that
is guaranteed by the Constitution." And the right to disseminate
such information may be abridged only "where the clear danger
of substantive evils arises under circumstances affording no opportunity to test the merits of ideas by competition for acceptance
in the market of public opinion." Here the danger to the industrial
concern was neither so serious nor so imminent as to warrant
the sweeping interference with freedom of discussion that the
statute prescribed.

In the Carlson case the Court, speaking through Mr. Justice
Murphy, held that the display of signs and banners was a natural
and appropriate method of publicizing the facts of a labor controversy, and that it is consequently a part of freedom of the press
protected against the action of the state by the Fourteenth Amendment.

Although these cases extended the protection of the Fourteenth
Amendment to peaceful picketing as a form of free speech or
press, they did not purport to free it from all restraint. The following term a sharply divided Supreme Court ruled that peaceful
picketing may be enjoined if the labor dispute has been attended
by serious and widespread violence. In *Milk Wagon Drivers
Union* v. *Meadowmoor Dairies*,[5] the Court was confronted with
the application of the Thornhill rule to the more complicated
situation of a milk-wagon drivers' strike in Chicago.

The case involved an injunction which had been secured by
the dairy to restrain the union from interfering with the distribution of its milk. The Supreme Court of the United States, in an
opinion by Mr. Justice Frankfurter, sustained this injunction. He
found that the past violence had "given to the picketing a coercive
effect" and that "acts which in isolation are peaceful may be part of
a coercive thrust when entangled with acts of violence." In such
a setting, "it could justifiably be concluded that the momentum
of fear generated by past violence would survive even though
future picketing might be wholly peaceful."

[5] 312 U.S. 287 (1941).

On the same day on which the Meadowmoor case was decided, the Court held that a state might not lawfully enjoin picketing because the picketers were not parties to an immediate labor dispute.[6] Justice Frankfurter declared in support of this conclusion that "A state cannot exclude workingmen from peacefully exercising the right of free communication by drawing the circle of economic competition between employers and workers so small as to contain only an employer and those directly employed by him."

The following year, in *Carpenters' and Joiners' Union* v. *Ritter's Cafe*,[7] the Court seemed to retreat somewhat from the broad principle laid down in the Thornhill case. In this case the union had been enjoined, under the Texas antitrust law, from picketing Ritter's restaurant because nonunion workers were employed by a contractor who was erecting a building for Ritter in another part of the city of Houston. The Texas court held that the picketing, which was peaceful, was being unlawfully carried on at a place remote from the scene of the actual dispute. Since the picketing took place at Ritter's restaurant rather than at the place where the building was being erected, it constituted an unlawful interference with his business. Mr. Justice Frankfurter, speaking for the majority of five, upheld the Texas court, and held that the union's right of free speech was not impaired by the injunction. His words were: "The recognition of peaceful picketing as an exercise of free speech does not imply that the states must be without power to confine the sphere of communication to that directly related to the dispute."

On its face, this statement seems inconsistent with the rationalization of Mr. Frankfurter in the preceding case. The line of distinction drawn by the Court seems to be this: Here "Texas has deemed it desirable to insulate from the dispute an establishment which industrially has no connection with the dispute." The state has made no effort to safeguard other building enterprises of the contractor. In the Swing case, on the other hand, the circle was drawn around the employer and his immediate employees in the same industry. Hence "the circle of economic competition"

[6] *American Federation of Labor* v. *Swing,* 312 U.S. 321 (1941).
[7] 315 U.S. 722 (1942).

may not be drawn between an employer and his immediate employees but may be drawn between discrete industries.

In 1943, however, in *Cafeteria Employees Union* v. *Angelos*,[8] the rule of the Thornhill case was extended to enterprises that had no employees.

Although the Thornhill doctrine had been mildly curtailed in the Meadowmoor and Ritter cases, its most serious shrinkage was produced by a series of cases in which the Court elaborated the principle that a state may forbid peaceful picketing conducted in violation of valid state law. The first of these cases was that of *Giboney* v. *Empire Storage and Ice Co.*,[9] in which the Court unanimously held that the state of Missouri might enjoin peaceful picketing that was designed to force the picketed persons to violate the valid antitrade-restraint law of the state. The avowed purpose of the picketing was to compel the ice company to agree to stop selling ice to nonunion peddlers in violation of the aforementioned statute.

The union's contention that the injunction against picketing adjacent to Empire's place of business was an unwarranted abridgment of its freedom of speech in attempting peacefully to publicize truthful facts about a labor dispute elicited from Mr. Justice Black this declaration for the unanimous Court: "It rarely has been suggested that constitutional freedom for speech and press extends its immunity to speech or writing used as an integral part of conduct in violation of a valid criminal statute. We reject the contention now." Furthermore, this rule applies even where the public policy of the state is determined by the rulings of a court rather than by the legislature.

Three cases decided in the 1949 term of the Court further limited the right to picket as an element of freedom of speech. In *Hughes* v. *Superior Court of California*,[10] the Court held that the Fourteenth Amendment does not bar a state from the use of the injunction to restrain picketing of a place of business solely in order to force compliance with a demand that its employees be apportioned according to the racial origin of its customers. The

[8] 320 U.S. 293 (1943).
[9] 336 U.S. 490 (1949).
[10] 339 U.S. 460 (1950).

demand was contrary to the policy of the state of California against racial discrimination in employment.

In *Building Service Employees International Union* v. *Gazzam*,[11] the Supreme Court held that the state of Washington might enjoin peaceful picketing designed to compel an employer to coerce his employees into joining the picketing union, in violation of the statutorily declared policy of the state that employers shall not coerce their employees' choice of a bargaining representative. The most significant of these cases was that of *International Teamsters Union* v. *Hanke*,[12] for here the picketing union was making no unlawful demands. The Court sustained a Washington state court injunction restraining picketing of businesses operated by the owners themselves without other employees for the purpose of compelling the observance of opening and closing hours set by the union. Once more, the Court declared through Justice Frankfurter that

. . . while picketing has an ingredient of communication, it cannot dogmatically be equated with the constitutionally protected freedom of speech. . . . The effort in the cases has been to strike a balance between the constitutional protection of the element of communication in picketing and "the power of the state to set the limits of permissible contest open to industrial combatants."

It seems clear that the ingredient of speech in this combination was substantially diminished in this case. To accomplish this required a narrow and ingenious construction of some earlier cases.[13] These cases, according to Justice Frankfurter, merely established the rule "that a state could not proscribe picketing merely by setting artificial bounds, unreal in the light of modern circumstances, to what constitutes an industrial relationship or a labor dispute."[14] Although this case did not specifically overrule the Thornhill case, it is clear that it divested it of much of its constitutional vitality.

What, then, is the present status of picketing as freedom of

[11] 339 U.S. 532 (1950).
[12] 339 U.S. 470 (1950).
[13] *Senn* v. *Tile Layers Protective Union*, 301 U.S. 468 (1937); see also notes 6 and 9.
[14] 339 U.S. 470, 479–80 (1950).

expression? First, it is still true that indiscriminate curbing of peaceful picketing, by statute or injunction, is a denial of free speech in violation of the due process clause of the Fourteenth Amendment. But picketing is more than speech; it is an economic weapon, and as such it is subject to extensive regulation by the state with respect to both its methods and its purposes. Thus, for example, peaceful picketing may be restrained when conducted in a context of violence or when it is designed to thwart a validly declared state policy, whether the declaration emanates from the legislature or from the courts.

It is difficult to piece together from the foregoing cases any judicial philosophy, formula, or standard which has predictive value. "The essence of the problem of the picketing cases is to draw a line between the unquestioned privilege to discuss industrial relations freely and the far more limited right to exert the economic power of an organized group of workers held together by union discipline."[15] Peaceful picketing directed primarily to the general public is one thing, but peaceful picketing for the purpose of compelling an employer to violate a valid state policy is quite another thing. To hold the latter valid would be to give speech by means of picketing a preferred position over the more traditional forms of free speech.

Finally, it should also be noted that the institution of the closed shop is not entitled to the protection of the *due process* clause of the Fourteenth Amendment as an incident of the right of employees to assemble and associate together in labor organizations. In *Lincoln Labor Union* v. *Northwestern Iron & Metal Co.*,[16] the Court declared that "The constitutional right of workers to assembly, to discuss and formulate plans for furthering their own self-interest in jobs cannot be construed as a constitutional guarantee that none shall get and hold jobs except those who will join in the assembly or will agree to abide by the assembly's plans."

[15] Archibald Cox, "Strikes, Picketing and the Constitution," *Vanderbilt Law Review*, Vol. 4 (April, 1951), p. 599.

[16] 355 U.S. 525, 531 (1949). See also *Auto Workers* v. *Wisconsin Employment Relations Board*, 336 U.S. 245 (1949); *American Federation of Labor* v. *American Sash and Door Co.*, 335 U.S. 538 (1949).

Judicial Restraint: Contempt of Court

In a series of three cases [17] decided between 1941 and 1947, the Court held that discussion of pending litigation or criticism of past decisions was punishable by contempt procedure only in the face of a clear and present danger to the fair administration of justice. In none of these cases was the danger to the obstruction of justice so serious or so imminent as to warrant the restraint of freedom of speech and press. Nevertheless, in a more recent case,[18] which involved contempt committed by an attorney in the physical presence of the Court, it was held that summary conviction and punishment were no denial of due process, even though the attorney's remarks were induced by "mildly provocative language from the bench."

In three of the preceding cases the Court was sharply divided, but despite this diversity among the justices, the general right of the press and of individuals to comment on and criticize pending judicial proceedings, as well as past judicial acts, seems well established. In determining whether a publication seriously threatens the administration of justice, consideration is given the supposition that the judge is a man "of reasonable fortitude" and is possessed of "a serenity that keeps him above the battle and the crowd."

Generally speaking, the position of the Court that wider judicial latitude should be permitted in the case of contempt committed in the immediate physical presence of the Court would seem to be sensible. Contempt committed in the face of the judge presents a clearer and more imminent danger to the calm and unprejudiced administration of justice than does printed criticism from a point outside the courtroom.

Since all four cases involved state courts, it should be noted that the power of the federal courts to punish for contempt is limited by Congressional statutes to misconduct in the presence of the courts, "or so near thereto as to obstruct the administration of justice," and the latest holding of the Supreme Court is that

[17] *Bridges* v. *California,* 314 U.S. 252 (1941); *Pennekamp* v. *Florida,* 378 U.S. 331 (1946); *Craig* v. *Harney,* 331 U.S. 367 (1947).
[18] *Fisher* v. *Pace,* 336 U.S. 155 (1949).

the word *near* indicates proximity in space and not a causal relationship.[19]

The conflict of interests presented in such cases as these confronts the Court with a dilemma, for there is involved a conflict not merely between public authority and private right but also between two important individual rights—the right to freedom of expression and the right to a fair and impartial trial by a court unimpeded by external pressure. In resolving the dilemma, the Court gave priority to freedom of expression because "the liberties of the First Amendment . . . are too highly prized to be subjected to the hazards of summary contempt procedure."

Freedom of Speech in Public Parks and Streets

The expansion of the area of judicial protection of civil liberties since the early 1930's has been especially notable with respect to the protection afforded those who wish to use the public parks and streets as forums for public discussion and the dissemination of propaganda. The extent of this development is strikingly illustrated by two Supreme Court cases separated by a period of 42 years. In the first case, decided in 1897, the Court unanimously sustained an ordinance of the city of Boston, providing that "no person shall, in or upon any of the public grounds, make any public address . . . except in accordance with a permit of the mayor." Here, the Court took the position that for the legislature to forbid public speaking in a public park or highway was no more a violation of the rights of a member of the public than would be the refusal of the owner of a private house to permit it in his house.[20] In 1939 the Court held void on its face an ordinance of Jersey City, N. J., because it allowed the Director of Safety to refuse permits for public meetings on the basis of his opinion that such refusal would prevent riots, disorderly assemblages, or other disturbances.[21]

Distribution of "literature." In an interesting series of cases beginning in 1938, the right under the due process clause of the

[19] *Nye* v. *United States*, 313 U.S. 33 (1941); see also *Toledo Newspaper Co.* v. *United States*, 247 U.S. 402 (1918).

[20] *Davis* v. *Massachusetts*, 167 U.S. 43 (1897).

[21] *Hague* v. *C.I.O.*, 307 U.S. 496 (1939).

Fourteenth Amendment to distribute books, pamphlets, or leaflets on city streets and other public places without prior official permission or payment of a license tax was sustained as the proper exercise of freedom of the press. Parenthetically, it should be stated here that most of these cases also involve questions of religious freedom, and will receive further consideration in Chapter 4.

The first of the handbill cases was that of *Lovell* v. *Griffin*,[22] in which the Court invalidated a municipal ordinance of the city of Griffin, Ga., which forbade the distribution of all "literature," in whatever form and whether sold or given away, without the written permission of the City Manager. Lovell had been convicted, fined, and jailed for the distribution of religious tracts in violation of the ordinance. On appeal, the Supreme Court, through Chief Justice Hughes, held the ordinance invalid on its face, since "it strikes at the very foundation of the freedom of the press by subjecting it to license and censorship." Furthermore, the liberty of the press is not confined to newspapers and periodicals but embraces also pamphlets and leaflets. These, indeed, have been the historic weapons wielded in defense of liberty, as the pamphlets of Thomas Paine and others in our own fight for freedom abundantly attest. In its historical connotation, the press includes every form of publication which affords a medium of information and opinion. Moreover, freedom of the press extends to distribution of printed matter by persons other than the authors. Without freedom of circulation, publication would be of little value.

In subsequent cases the constitutional protection afforded the distribution of printed matter in streets and other public places was reaffirmed and extended to other situations. In *Schneider* v. *Irvington*[23] four cases involving the validity of municipal ordinances in four cities in as many states were merged. All the ordinances forbade the distribution of handbills in the streets or other public places; the Irvington ordinance went further and provided that "no one without a permit from the chief of police shall canvass, solicit, distribute circulars, or other matter, or call from house to house." Here was presented for the determination of the Court a sharp conflict between the traditional police power of the states to regulate in order to maintain the cleanliness, convenience, and

[22] 303 U.S. 444 (1938).   [23] 308 U.S. 147 (1939).

good order of city streets and the fundamental right of freedom of the press. The ordinances were defended as reasonable police regulations to prevent littering of the streets and to protect the residents from the annoyance and danger of unrequested canvassing. With Mr. Justice McReynolds alone dissenting, the Court held all the ordinances void, as abridging freedom of speech and press guaranteed against the states by the Fourteenth Amendment. Said Justice Roberts for the Court: "Although a municipality may enact regulations in the interest of public safety, health, welfare or convenience, these may not abridge the individual liberties secured by the Constitution to those who wish to speak, write, print or circulate information or opinion." Certainly, cities have a duty to keep their streets clean and free from obstruction, but to accomplish this end they may not forbid a person rightfully on the street from handing "literature" to one willing to receive it. In some of these cases, recipients had thrown the leaflets on the sidewalk and the street with resultant littering of the street. Such offenders can undoubtedly be punished in the interest of preserving cleanliness and order in the streets, but this end may not be achieved by abridgment of those "fundamental rights and liberties," the "exercise of which lies at the foundation of free government by free men."

The Irvington, N. J., ordinance restricting house-to-house canvassing, which was not limited to commercial canvassing, was violated by a person distributing religious tracts and was held by the Supreme Court to impose a prior censorship on the distribution of literature and the communication of opinion. This censorship, being subject to imposition at the discretion of police officials, makes the ordinance permitting it a violation of both free speech and free press. In *Martin* v. *Struthers*[24] in 1943, the same constitutional protection was successfully invoked against an ordinance making it unlawful for a distributor of handbills, circulars, or other advertising matter to ring door bells or knock on doors in order to summon the occupant to the door for the purpose of receiving such matter.

The Court pointed out that the dangers and abuses of this method of distribution can be easily "controlled by traditional

[24] 319 U.S. 141 (1943).

legal methods," such as a regulation making it unlawful to ring the door bell of any householder who has appropriately warned that he is not to be disturbed. Thus, in *Breard* v. *Alexandria* [25] the Court sustained an ordinance forbidding door-to-door solicitation without the prior consent of the owners of the residences. Here constitutionality of the regulation depended "upon a balancing of the conveniences between some householders' desire for privacy and the publisher's right to distribute publications in the precise way that those soliciting for him think brings the best results."

This case was distinguished from the Struthers case on the ground that no commercial element was involved in the latter. The ordinance here covered only commercial advertising. It had previously been held that the right to distribute information or propagandist literature upon the public streets does not extend to commercial advertising. This is true even where commercial handbills carry a "public protest," which taken alone would be insurance from the restriction. [26]

The foregoing principle was extended even to the right to distribute religious literature in a company-owned town [27] or within a federal housing development without permission of the owners. [28]

In two other cases, the Supreme Court, reversing a previous decision, [29] held invalid municipal license taxes imposed on those who sell or distribute religious literature on the streets or from house to house [30] as previous restraint on freedom of the press and the free exercise of religion. Although such a tax may be imposed upon peddlers of nonreligious publications or other goods, religious activity may not be taxed at all. It enjoys a "preferred position" of complete immunity. This rule applies even to a person who makes his living entirely from the sale of religious books. [31]

Sound trucks. The two well-known sound truck cases show that technological progress can have a far-reaching and confusing

[25] 341 U.S. 622 (1951).
[26] *Valentine* v. *Christensen*, 316 U.S. 52 (1942).
[27] *Marsh* v. *Alabama*, 326 U.S. 501 (1946).
[28] *Tucker* v. *Texas*, 326 U.S. 517 (1946).
[29] *Jones* v. *Opelika*, 316 U.S. 584 (1942).
[30] *Murdock* v. *Pennsylvania*, 319 U.S. 105 (1943).
[31] *Follett* v. *McCormick*, 321 U.S. 573 (1944); see also later cases in which the Court condemned licensing systems to control speech: *Kunz* v. *New York*, 340 U.S. 290, and *Niemotko* v. *Maryland*, 340 U.S. 268 (1951).

effect upon the constitutional right of the individual to freedom of expression, as well as upon the power of government to regulate commerce and industry. The question presented here was whether the freedom of expression long afforded the natural voice applied to speech amplified by an electronic apparatus.

In the first of these cases a city ordinance of Lockport, N. Y., forbidding the use of sound amplification devices in public places, except with the permission of the chief of police, and prescribing no standards for the exercise of his discretion, was held unconstitutional on its face, since it established a previous restraint on the right of free speech in violation of the First Amendment made applicable to the states through the Fourteenth Amendment.[32] As indicated, the chief objection noted by the five-man majority was the absence of any standards defining the discretion of the chief of police. Furthermore, free speech protection extends to loudspeakers, declared Mr. Justice Douglas, because they "are today indispensable instruments of effective public speech. The sound truck has become an accepted method of political campaigning. It is the way people are reached."

Finally Justice Douglas pointed out that, although courts in passing on the constitutionality of local regulations of the kind involved here must balance the various community interests, they should in that process "be mindful to keep the freedoms of the First Amendment in a preferred position."

Eight months after this decision another majority of five, comprising the former dissenters and Chief Justice Vinson, upheld the provision of a Trenton, N. J., ordinance making it unlawful for anyone to operate, for any purpose on the public streets, sound trucks or any amplifying device attached to a vehicle "emitting loud and raucous noises."[33] This ordinance, written in awkward and ambiguous language, is on its face more stringent than the Lockport ordinance, for it appears to be, in effect, a complete prohibition of electronic apparatus. Indeed, it was so interpreted by the state courts.[34] Nevertheless the new court majority held it

[32] *Saia v. New York*, 334 U.S. 558, 562 (1948).
[33] *Kovacs v. Cooper*, 336 U.S. 77 (1949).
[34] See C. H. Pritchett, *Civil Liberties and the Vinson Court* (Chicago, University of Chicago Press, 1954), p. 45.

to be a permissible exercise of legislative discretion to bar sound trucks with broadcasts of public interest, amplified to a loud and raucous volume, from the public ways of a municipality.

The judgment of the Court was announced by Justice Reed in an opinion which had the support of only the Chief Justice and Justice Burton. In the view of these three, the words *loud* and *raucous* were not so vague as to deny due process of law. The case was distinguished from Saia on the dubious mechanical basis that the Trenton ordinance, unlike the Lockport ordinance, did not vest uncontrolled discretion in the chief of police. The Justice failed to point out that the Lockport ordinance at least insured the discussion of certain matters through loud-speakers, subject to permission by the chief of police. Justice Reed, however, insisted that the Trenton ordinance did not abridge the right guaranteed to every citizen to reach the mind of willing listeners and that "unrestrained use throughout a municipality of all sound amplification devices would be intolerable." Thus, he would seem to rest the decision upon the "loud and raucous" test, but this was not accepted by a majority of the justices. It is not clear, then, whether sound trucks not emitting loud and raucous noises may be barred from the parks and streets.

Justices Jackson and Frankfurter, concurring, did not accept the loud and raucous test and apparently construed the ordinance to ban all sound trucks. Jackson agreed with Justice Black, who dissented, that the Saia decision struck down a more moderate exercise of the state's police power than the one here sustained and that this decision repudiates Saia. However, he thought that sound amplifying devices could be constitutionally regulated to any extent short of censorship of the contents of the broadcast. Justice Frankfurter thought that the terms on which sound trucks may be permitted to operate, if at all, should be left to the legislative judgment, so long as the legislature does not prescribe the ideas that may be noisily expressed or not expressed, nor discriminate among those who would thus disturb the public peace.

The sharp diversity of opinion among the justices of the Court in these two sound truck cases leaves the constitutional status of this new medium of communication unsettled and confused.

As C. H. Pritchett aptly observes,[35] "Justice Reed achieved the dubious distinction in the Kovacs case of writing an opinion for the Court to which five Justices objected, and of upholding a conviction on a different interpretation of local law from that of the state courts."

At best only tentative conclusions can be drawn from these decisions. It is apparent that in general the use of sound amplifying devices is entitled to the protection of freedom of expression guaranteed by the Fourteenth Amendment, but volume of sound, time of broadcasting, and other conditions may be regulated by "narrowly drawn ordinances." An ordinance vesting arbitrary licensing power in a municipal official is clearly unconstitutional. But other cases will have to be decided before it is possible to say precisely how free speech doctrine applies to sound trucks.

Right of Privacy in Public Places

Although it is constitutional for a municipal ordinance to forbid "loud and raucous noises" from a sound truck on public streets, on the theory that "such distractions would be dangerous to traffic" and disturbing of the "quiet and tranquility so desirable for city-dwellers," there is no constitutional objection to the converse procedure of a street railway company amplifying radio programs through loud speakers in its passenger cars. The Public Utilities Commission of the District of Columbia, after an investigation and public hearings, issued an order permitting the Capital Transit Company, over the protest of some of its patrons, to receive and amplify radio programs consisting generally of 90 per cent music, 5 per cent announcements, and 5 per cent commercial advertising. The Court held that neither the operation of the radio service nor the action of the Commission permitting its operation is precluded by the federal Constitution.[36] In this connection Justice Burton emphasized the fact that an overwhelming majority of the passengers had approved of the programs.

Justice Douglas dissented on the ground that the practice of forcing people to listen to a radio program violated the due process

---

[35] *Ibid.*, p. 46.
[36] *Public Utilities Commission of the District of Columbia* v. *Pollak*, 343 U.S. 451 (1952).

right to privacy, which is, he asserted, "the beginning of all freedom."

Justice Reed had declared in the Kovacs case that "The right of free speech is guaranteed every citizen that he may reach the minds of willing listeners." But this apparently does not apply to those on the receiving end in a public place. In short, there is no right of privacy in a public place.

Motion Pictures and Freedom of Communication

In 1952, the Supreme Court finally came to grips with the issue of motion picture censorship, which had long since become widely established. In 1915, the Court had held that a state law providing for the censorship of motion pictures was valid, on the theory that the showing of motion pictures is "a business pure and simple, originated and conducted for profit," and "not to be regarded as a part of the press of the country or as organs of public opinion."[37] This was long before the Court had become greatly concerned with civil liberties issues, and in 1948 the Court said by way of a dictum in a case involving another issue: "We have no doubt that motion pictures, like newspapers and radio, are included in the press whose freedom is guaranteed by the First Amendment."[38]

This dictum became the basis of the Court's ruling against motion picture censorship in the so-called "Miracle case" in 1952.[39] In this case, provisions of the New York Education Law which forbid the showing of any motion picture film without a license, and authorize denial of a license on a censor's conclusion that a film is "sacrilegious," were held invalid as a prior restraint on freedom of speech and press under the Fourteenth Amendment. "It cannot be doubted," wrote Justice Clark for the unanimous Court, "that motion pictures are a significant medium for the communication of ideas" in many different ways, and their importance "is not lessened by the fact that they are designed to entertain as well as to inform." Nor does it matter, contrary to the position of the Court in Mutual Film Corporation, that the motion picture

---

[37] *Mutual Film Corporation* v. *Industrial Commission,* 237 U.S. 230, 244 (1915).
[38] *United States* v. *Paramount Pictures, Inc.,* 334 U.S. 131, 166 (1948).
[39] *Joseph Burstyn* v. *Wilson,* 343 U.S. 495 (1952).

enterprise is a large-scale business conducted for private profit. The fact that books, papers, and magazines are published and sold for profit does not prevent them from being a form of expression safeguarded by the First Amendment. The Court sees no reason why operation for profit should alter the circumstances for motion pictures. It apparently had had a different effect in some of the handbill cases previously discussed.[40]

One week later, a Texas decision sustaining an ordinance of the city of Marshall, which authorized a board of censors "to deny a license for the showing of any motion picture which in its opinion is of such a character as to be prejudicial to the best interest of the people" of the city, was reversed *per curiam* without opinion on the authority of the Burstyn case and *Winters* v. *New York*, a decision in which a New York criminal statute had been invalidated on the ground of vagueness. Justice Frankfurter in a brief statement seemed to concur solely on the score of indefiniteness, but Justice Douglas in a concurring statement completely ignored the vagueness issue and saw prior restraint present in "a flagrant form" as the basis of invalidity. "If a board of censors can tell the American people what it is in their best interest to see or to read or to hear, then thought is regimented, authority substituted for liberty, and the great purpose of the First Amendment to keep uncontrolled the freedom of expression defeated."[41]

Early in 1954, in a *per curiam* opinion[42] the Court reversed judgments of the Court of Appeals of New York and the Supreme Court of Ohio, sustaining, respectively, a New York statute prohibiting the public showing of motion pictures "which were immoral" or which would "tend to corrupt morals," and an Ohio statute prohibiting the public exhibition of motion pictures which were not of a "moral, educational or amusing and harmless character." The New York case involved the refusal of a license for the showing of a motion picture entitled *La Ronde*, and the Ohio case, the denial of a license for a film called *M*. In its unanimous reversal, the Supreme Court of the United States merely cited

[40] *Valentine* v. *Christensen*, 316 U.S. 52, and *Breard* v. *Alexandria*, 341 U.S. 622.

[41] *Gelling* v. *Texas*, 343 U.S. 960, 961 (1952).

[42] *Superior Films, Inc.* v. *Dept. of Education*, 346 U.S. 587 (1954).

the Burstyn case as authority. Thus the question of the standards of permissible censorship of motion pictures is still unresolved. Indeed, in the light of these opinions it would seem to be uncertain whether a majority of the Court has found motion picture censorship invalid as a matter of principle or merely where standards of guilt are too vague. At any rate, further litigation will be necessary to clarify the status of this relatively new medium of communication with respect to the liberty of expression guaranteed by the First and Fourteenth Amendments.

The Police Power: Public Order and Public Morals

Perhaps the most extreme and divergent application of the clear and present danger test to uphold or deny libertarian claims relates to exercise of the state police power to maintain public order and safety and to protect public morality. It is, of course, clear that not all speech is protected under the First and Fourteenth Amendments. In *Chaplinsky* v. *New Hampshire*,[43] a case in which the conviction of the petitioner, under a New Hampshire statute providing that "no person shall address any offensive, derisive or annoying word to any person who is lawfully in any street or other public place, nor call him by any offensive or derisive name," etc., was sustained, Mr. Justice Murphy made this statement:

> There are certain well-defined and narrowly limited classes of speech, the prevention and punishment of which have never been thought to raise any constitutional problem. These include the lewd and obscene, the profane, the libelous, and the insulting or "fighting" words—those which by their very utterance inflict injury or tend to incite an immediate breach of the peace. It has been well observed that such are no essential part of any exposition of ideas, and are of such slight social value as a step to truth that any benefit that may be derived from them is clearly outweighed by the social interest in order and morality.

This was the view generally followed by the Court before application of the clear and present danger test to such situations in the 1940's. Nevertheless, Justice Douglas, with little consideration of the facts of the case, set forth an absolutist conception of

[43] 315 U.S. 568, 571, 572 (1942).

free speech in *Terminiello* v. *Chicago*[44] in 1949, which was calculated seriously to restrict the power of local government to maintain public order. The Court by a 5 to 4 vote reversed a conviction under an ordinance which, as interpreted by the Municipal Court, permitted punishment for breach of the peace of speech which "stirs the public to anger, invites disputes, brings about a condition of unrest, or creates a disturbance." The case stemmed from an extremely inflammatory address by an irrepressible rabble-rouser, attacking in a long string of insulting and fighting epithets the members of various racial and political groups and government officials, in an auditorium guarded by the police from a threatening mob on the outside. Apparently rejecting the "fighting words" theory of the Chaplinsky case, Justice Douglas wrote for the narrow majority that "A function of free speech under our system of government is to invite dispute," and that it may serve its purpose best when it "induces a condition of unrest . . . or even stirs people to anger." For this reason, the Justice concluded, "freedom of speech, though not absolute . . . is nevertheless protected against censorship or punishment, unless shown likely to produce a clear and present danger of a serious substantive evil that rises far above public convenience, annoyance, or unrest."

In a hard-hitting dissenting opinion, Justice Jackson argued that the Court had abandoned the conception of "fighting words" and "clear and present danger" embodied in earlier cases and had substituted in their place "a dogma of absolute freedom for irresponsible and provocative utterance which almost completely sterilizes the power of local authorities to keep the peace against this kind of tactics." He concluded with the observation that the Court had gone far toward "accepting the doctrine that civil liberty means the removal of all restraints from these crowds" and with the warning to his brethren that, "if the Court does not temper its doctrinaire logic with a little practical wisdom, it will convert the constitutional Bill of Rights into a suicide pact."

It is difficult to reconcile the position of the Court in this case with the holding in *Feiner* v. *New York*,[45] decided early in 1951.

[44] 337 U.S. 1, 4 (1949).
[45] 340 U.S. 315 (1951).

Feiner, a university student, made a speech from a box on a street corner in Syracuse, N. Y., in which he applied the appellation *bum* to the President of the United States and to several lesser officials. It was also alleged, but disputed, that he urged the Negroes in his audience to rise up in arms and fight for their rights. It was generally agreed that the speaker stirred up "a little excitement." When one of his auditors, with the aid of an epithet reflecting on Feiner's ancestry, threatened violence against him if the police did not pull him down from the box, the police intervened and, after two unheeded requests that Feiner stop speaking, arrested him on a charge of disorderly conduct. He was later convicted by the local trial court, and the conviction was affirmed by two state appellate courts. Relying upon the findings of these state courts that danger to public order was theatened, the Supreme Court of the United States, through Chief Justice Vinson, expressed confidence that the arrest had been made solely "for the preservation of order and protection of the general welfare," and with no thought of curbing the expression of the petitioner's opinions. It is significant that the Chief Justice explicitly stated that Feiner was not arrested or convicted for what he said but rather because of the reaction of some of his listeners to the speech. Feiner was nevertheless found guilty of inciting to riot and of deliberately defying police officers and was sent to prison. This is, indeed, a hazardous formula for those who would exercise their freedom of speech on street corners. Police suppression is simply dependent upon the willingness of someone in the audience to create a disturbance.

Justice Black thought that the policeman's action in arresting Feiner without explanation was a "deliberate defiance" of official duty, as well as of the constitutional right of free speech.

Justice Douglas, also in dissent, argued that it was the duty of the police to protect Feiner from the threatening auditor, and that by failing to do so they threw their weight on the side of those who sought to break up the meeting, thereby becoming "the new censors of speech."

In the field of public morality, the Court held invalid in *Winters*

v. *United States*[46] the exercise of the police power of the State of New York in a statute which made it a crime to "print, publish or distribute . . . any printed matter principally made up of criminal views, or pictures or stories of deeds of bloodshed, lust, or crime." The state courts construed the statute "as prohibiting such massing of accounts of deeds of bloodshed and lust as to incite to crimes against the person." Even as thus construed, the Supreme Court by a 6 to 3 vote held the act invalid on the ground that it was so vague and indefinite as to violate procedural due process under the Fourteenth Amendment. It did not define the forbidden acts with such precision as to exclude a legitimate exercise of the right of free speech and press. Why the Court could not trust itself to strike down such encroachments upon these freedoms when presented to it is not made clear.

Justice Frankfurter, in a dissenting opinion in which Justices Burton and Jackson joined, respectfully suggested that the Court had been led into error, by confusing the lack of certainty with respect to the outcome of different prosecutions for similar conduct with the lack of definiteness in the prohibition of the law. The former uncertainties will remain so long as judges are fallible, but they do not deprive persons of due process of law.

On the other hand, such terms as *obscene* and *lewd* may be employed in a criminal statute because, through a long history in the law, they have presumably acquired a reasonably definite meaning. Nevertheless, the Court experiences extreme difficulty in the determination of cases involving censorship or punishment of obscene publications. And oddly enough this difficulty springs from the virtual impossibility of defining obscenity. Cases decided in the 1956 term of the Court illustrate this difficulty.

In *Roth* v. *United States*[47] and *Alberts* v. *California*, combined for the hearing, the Court decided that obscenity is not protected by the First Amendment against federal proscription, nor by the due process clause of the Fourteenth Amendment against state proscription. This is true because obscenity, like libel, is bad in itself, and therefore does not fall within the protection of free

[46] 333 U.S. 507, 514–15, 535 (1948).
[47] 354 U.S. 476 (1957).

expression under the clear and present danger test. Obscene expressions are in the nature of verbal action and by their very utterance inflict harm upon those to whom they are addressed. Consequently, they may be punished without regard to probable effect upon the conduct of others.

Justice Brennan, for the Court, found the ". . . rejection of obscenity as utterly without redeeming social importance," and he concluded that material which tends to incite lustful thoughts may be suppressed without evidence that it will probably lead to antisocial conduct. The test of obscenity applied was "whether to the average person, applying contemporary community standards, the dominant theme of the material taken as a whole appeals to prurient interest." This was deemed to define obscenity with sufficient clarity so that the constitutionally protected area for discussion of sex, which is not to be confused with obscenity, would be adequately safeguarded.

It was on this standard that the Court in *Roth* v. *United States* sustained a federal statute forbidding the transportation through the mails of "obscene, lewd, lascivious, indecent, filthy or vile" materials, and in *Alberts* v. *California* a statute forbidding the writing or production of "obscene or indecent" matter. Thus, in these cases the Court decided for the first time that a "sufficiently explicit" obscenity statute was constitutional.[48]

Justice Harlan, dissenting in Roth, thought the Court's sweeping generalization about obscenity's being outside constitutional protection begged the question before the Court. He would have had the Court construe the federal statute, in order to make it constitutional, as reaching only "hard-core pornography." He found that the material here involved did not qualify under his test.

In *Butler* v. *Michigan*,[49] a statute which defined as a misdemeanor making available to the general reading public any book containing obscene language, "tending to the corruption of the morals of youth," was struck down by the Court because it was "not reasonably restricted to the evil with which it is said to deal."

[48] See *Doubleday & Co.* v. *New York,* 335 U.S. 848 (1948).
[49] 352 U.S. 380 (1957).

Adults may not be restricted to reading matter fit only for children. "Surely," said Justice Frankfurter, "this is to burn the house to roast the pig."

RIGHT OF ASSEMBLY AND PETITION

Nature of the Right

One of the basic rights of every American under the First Amendment and the due process clause of the Fourteenth Amendment of the Constitution is the right to assemble with others for the purpose of discussing problems of common interest and of protesting against actions and policies of government deemed to be unjust, or unwise, or calling for positive action by government deemed to be in the public interest.

Throughout a large part of its history the right of petition was regarded as primary to the right of assembly, the latter being a subordinate and ancillary right. Today, however, the right of assembly is fundamental. In *De Jonge* v. *Oregon,* the first case in which the right of assembly was held by the Supreme Court to be included in the "liberty" guaranteed against state abridgment by the due process clause of the Fourteenth Amendment, the Court declared that

peaceable assembly is a right cognate to those of free speech and free press and is equally fundamental. . . . For the right is one that cannot be denied without violating those fundamental principles of liberty and justice which lie at the base of all civil and political institutions—principles which the Fourteenth Amendment embodies in the general terms of its due process clause.

Therefore, the Court went on, "The holding of meetings for peaceable political action cannot be proscribed. Those who assist in the conduct of such meetings cannot be branded as criminals on that score." If the right of assembly is to be preserved, the question is not under whose auspices the meeting is held, but what is its purpose; not one of the relationship of the speakers, "but whether their utterances transcend the bounds of the freedom of speech which the Constitution protects."[50] Here, then, the Court flatly rejected the concept of guilt by association.

[50] *De Jonge* v. *Oregon,* 299 U.S. 353, 364, 365 (1937).

In the case from which these quotations come, De Jonge, a member of the Communist Party, was convicted in the state court for violation of the Oregon Syndicalism Act, which defined criminal syndicalism as "the doctrine which advocates crime, physical violence, sabotage, or any unlawful acts or methods as a means of accomplishing or effecting industrial or political change or revolution." The act also punishes various acts promotive of criminal syndicalism such as "presiding at or assisting in conducting a meeting of such an organization, society or group." On the undisputed evidence, De Jonge spoke at a meeting in Portland called by the Communist Party; he did not discuss criminal syndicalism but rather a current maritime strike. For this he was arrested, convicted, and sentenced to seven years in prison. Speaking through Chief Justice Hughes, the Supreme Court held that De Jonge had been deprived of freedom of assembly and speech without due process of law. The Court pointed out that under the interpretation which had been given the Oregon statute, no meeting of the Communist Party, however innocent the topic of discussion, would be lawful. This, held the Court, amounted to an arbitrary infringement of the right of freedom of assembly.

Federal Restraints

Attempts by government to regulate peaceful assembly of the people, as with freedom of speech and press, pose issues of sharp conflict between the importance of preserving freedom of communication and the necessity of maintaining public order and safety. The banning of such offenses as breach of peace, disorderly conduct, nuisances, and obstruction of public ways has operated to restrict the right of people to assemble for the exchange of ideas. To draw the line between legal and illegal regulation here is not always an easy task for the Court.

Restrictions by the national government have been less frequent in recent years than formerly.[51] Nevertheless, petitions for the repeal of the World War I espionage and sedition laws and against military recruitment have been punished by imprisonment. Es-

[51] See *The Constitution of the United States of America,* Annotated, 82d Cong., 2d Sess., Sen. Doc. 170 (Washington, Government Printing Office, 1953), pp. 806–807.

pecially unsuccessful have been processions or marches for the presentation of petitions in the national capital. In 1894 General Coxey's armies of unemployed marched on Washington, only to see their leaders arrested for walking on the grass around the Capitol. In 1932 the march of the veterans on Washington to petition for bonus legislation met with a stern rebuke. The Administration, considering the march a threat to the Constitution, called on the army to expel the bonus marchers from the capital and burn their camp.[52]

State Restraints

Before the doctrine of absorption of First Amendment freedoms into the concept of liberty guaranteed against state abridgment by the due process clause of the Fourteenth Amendment had been enunciated, it had been thought that there was no federal constitutional barrier to state or local regulation, or even prohibition, of meetings in public places. However, as has been seen, the existence of such a barrier was forecast in the Gitlow case in 1925 and definitely established for freedom of assembly in the De Jonge case in 1937.

One of the principal methods by which state and local governments have attempted to restrict meetings in public places has been requirement of a permit. Some of these regulations have been honest efforts to prevent interference with traffic, to give police protection to the gatherings when needed, or to maintain public order. At other times, however, the regulations have been rooted in prejudice and vindictiveness. On the whole, the Supreme Court has dealt sternly with the latter.

In *Hague* v. *C.I.O.*,[53] decided in 1939, the question at issue was the validity of a Jersey City, N. J., ordinance requiring a permit for public assemblies in the streets, parks, or public buildings of the city, and authorizing the Director of Public Safety to refuse to issue such a permit if, after investigation of all the facts and circumstances pertinent to the application, he believes it proper to refuse in order to prevent riots, disturbances, or disorderly assemblage.

[52] *Ibid.*
[53] 307 U.S. 496 (1939).

The Chief of Police of Jersey City, acting under the foregoing ordinance, denied the C.I.O. the right to hold lawful meetings in Jersey City on the alleged ground that the members were Communists or comprised communist organizations. When the case reached the Supreme Court, it was held by a majority of 5 to 2 that the ordinance was void on its face, since it allowed the Director of Public Safety to refuse permits for public meetings on his mere opinion that such refusal would prevent riots, disturbances, and disorderly assemblages.

In the principal opinion, Mr. Justice Roberts made this significant statement relative to the place of freedom of assembly in the American democratic system:

> Freedom of assembly is an essential element of the American democratic system. At the root of this case lies the question of the *value* in American life of the citizen's right to meet face to face with others for the discussion of their ideas and problems—religious, political, economic or social. Public debate and discussion take many forms including the spoken and the printed word, the radio and the screen. But assemblies face to face perform a function of vital significance in the American system, and are no less important at the present time for the education of the public and the formation of opinion than they have been in our past history. The right of assembly lies at the foundation of our system of government.

In *Bridges* v. *California* [54] it was held that a telegram sent to the Secretary of Labor, strongly assailing the action of a state court in a pending case, was entitled to protection under the Fourteenth Amendment as an exercise of the right of petition. In 1945, a state statute requiring union officials to register before soliciting union membership was found to violate the right of peaceful assembly. [55] A few years later, however, a closely divided Court sustained an order of a state employment relations board forbidding the calling of special union meetings during working hours, [56] and in June, 1951, the Court in a 6 to 3 decision held that a conspiracy to break up by force and threats of force a meeting called to protest against

[54] 314 U.S. 257 (1941).
[55] *Thomas* v. *Collins*, 323 U.S. 516 (1945).
[56] *Auto Workers* v. *Wisconsin Employment Relations Board*, 336 U.S. 245 (1949).

the Marshall Plan did not afford a right of action against the conspirators under the Ku Klux Klan Act of 1871.[57]

The three dissenters, speaking through Justice Burton, argued that Congress could punish a conspiracy of private persons that had as its purpose the denial of a federally created constitutional right.

Lobbying and the Right of Petition

Conflict of interest is again sharply involved in the widespread practice of lobbying, one of the most important expressions of the right of petition, and the persistent popular demand for restrictive regulation of this weapon of organized group interests. With the tremendous growth of organized special interest groups since the beginning of this century, the professional lobby has become the chief weapon of these groups for influencing governmental policy. Much criticism has developed concerning the methods and purposes of the organized interests, as they operate through their professional lobbyists.

Starting early in the present century, many states enacted legislation to regulate lobbyists. On the national level, there have been no less than four Congressional investigations of lobbying activities. A more recent one has been by a Committee of the House of Representatives authorized by the Eighty-first Congress in 1950.[58] In 1946 the Congress passed the Federal Regulation of Lobbying Act, under which more than 2000 lobbyists have registered and some 500 organizations have reported lobbying contributions and expenditures.

This act requires certain designated reports to be made to Congress by every person receiving contributions or expending money for the purpose of influencing, directly or indirectly, the passage or defeat of any legislation by Congress. The act also requires every person who engages, for pay or for any consideration, to attempt to influence the passage or defeat of any legislation by Congress to register with the Clerk of the House and the Secretary of the Senate and to make certain disclosures concerning himself and

[57] *Collins v. Hardyman*, 341 U.S. 651, 663 (1951).

[58] See *General Interim Report of the House Select Committee on Lobbying Activities*, 81st Cong., 2d Sess. (Washington, Government Printing Office, 1950).

his employer or the interest in whose behalf he is acting.[59]

In the case of *United States* v. *Rumely* decided in 1953, in which the Lobbying Act was indirectly involved, the Court ruled through Justice Frankfurter that "as a matter of English" the phrase "lobbying activities" means representations made directly "to Congress, its members or its committees" and does not embrace attempts to direct the thinking of the community. The next year, in *United States* v. *Harriss*,[60] the Court upheld the constitutionality of the act. Chief Justice Warren, referring to the Rumely case, argued that the language of the act was meant to refer to lobbying in the sense of "direct communication with members of Congress on pending or proposed federal legislation," and not to attempts to influence Congress indirectly through an appeal to public opinion.

Construed in this manner, the statute does not violate the First Amendment guarantees of free speech, press, and assembly. In support of this conclusion, the Chief Justice reasons that if the American ideal of government by elected representatives is to be fully realized, the individual members of Congress must be able to distinguish between the pressures of special interests "masquerading as proponents of the public weal" and the voice of the people. Congress by this legislation, he continues, is not seeking to forbid these pressures; it is seeking rather "a modicum of information" as to "who is being hired, who is putting up the money, and how much." To forbid Congress to do this is to deny it the power of self-protection.

SUMMARY ANALYSIS

Expansion of Scope of Protection

In the cases covered in this chapter, the exercise of freedom has, for the most part, collided with the police power of the state in fields of general welfare not closely related to the necessities of national security. In this sphere, the Court broadened the scope of protection of freedom to include new situations such as picketing, criticism of judicial conduct, the distribution of handbills and other printed materials in public places, the operation of sound

---

[59] 2 U.S.C. Sections 264, 266.   [60] 347 U.S. 612 (1954).

trucks in public places, and motion pictures. In the period and area discussed, the Court generally tended to give maximum scope to freedom.

Picketing. The Court in the initial case of *Thornhill* v. *Alabama* held that a statute which forbade all picketing, whether peaceful or not, was void on its face. It will be recalled that this holding was substantially modified in subsequent cases. However, picketing is still regarded as speech, and indiscriminate curbing of peaceful picketing is an unconstitutional restraint of freedom of speech. However, picketing is also an economic weapon and, as such, is subject to regulation by the state as to both methods and purposes. Thus peaceful picketing may be restrained if the labor dispute has in the past been attended by violence, extends beyond the industry involved in the dispute, or if its purpose is to force violation by the employer of a validly declared state policy.

Although the more recent cases have tended to minimize the element of speech in picketing and to accentuate the element of economic coercion, peaceful picketing directed primarily toward the purpose of informing the public of the facts of a labor dispute still enjoys the status and protection of free speech. The problem confronting the Court in picketing cases is that of drawing a line between the clear right to publicize and discuss industrial relations and the much more limited right of an organized group of workers to exert their economic power.

Contempt of Court. In a series of cases decided in the 1940's, the general right of the press and of individuals to criticize pending judicial proceedings, as well as past judicial acts, was upheld. Such a right, however, does not extend to contempt committed in the physical presence of the Court. The sharp division of the justices in this group of cases was no doubt due to the fact that they involve a conflict not merely between public authority and private right, but also between two important private rights, namely, freedom of expression and the right to a fair trial. The majority of the Court resolved the dilemma by the application of the doctrine of preferred status to freedom of expression.

Free speech in public places. The scope of free speech in public places was extended by a series of cases upholding the orderly distribution of handbills, phamphlets, and other materials on the streets and in other public places, and the sale of religious or non-commercial literature in public places, without prior official permission or payment of a license tax.

The most confusing and unsatisfactory aspect of this development involves the attempt to apply free speech doctrine to speech amplified by electronic devices. In the Saia case an ordinance requiring a license from the chief of police for the use of sound amplification devices was held to vest unrestrained discretion in the officer, and therefore amounted to previous restraint of speech. In Kovacs, the Court sustained an ordinance forbidding the operation of any sound truck emitting "loud and raucous" noises. Yet, part of the majority of five construed the ambiguous ordinance as banning all sound trucks. Hence it is impossible to say precisely what the application of free speech doctrine to sound trucks is. Wading through the confusing diversity of judicial opinion, we may tentatively state this much: Generally, the use of sound amplification devices is protected as freedom of expression by the Fourteenth Amendment, but volume of sound, time of broadcasting, and other conditions may be regulated by "narrowly drawn ordinances." An ordinance vesting unrestrained licensing power in an official is clearly invalid.

Motion pictures. In the case of the *Miracle* the Supreme Court extended the protection of freedom of expression to motion pictures. It will be recalled that up to the *Miracle* decision in 1952, there had been in force (since 1915) a decision that motion pictures are mere entertainment and not entitled to guarantees of freedom of expression. The *Miracle* ruling, holding invalid as prior restraint on freedom of expression the provision of a New York statute authorizing denial of a license to show a motion picture on a censor's judgment that the film is "sacrilegious," apparently does not preclude a state from censoring motion pictures "under a clearly drawn statute designed and applied to prevent the showing of obscene films."

Judicial Criteria

If there is any conclusion which emerges clearly from the foregoing consideration of free speech cases, it is that they have not been decided by the application of a tidy formula or even set of formulas. In every case the Court is confronted with a set of competing interests or values, and its decision will in the final analysis rest upon its evaluation of the relative importance of these conflicting interests, tempered by the several justices' conception of their proper judicial function. Hence, few generalizations are possible on the basis of these decisions, and predictions are hazardous. However, the following observations can be made with respect to the Court's handling of the free speech cases considered in this chapter:

In expanding the area of protection of freedom of expression to include new fields, the Court, as previously pointed out, gave wide scope to the exercise of freedom, and its most effective weapon in this battle was the clear and present danger test, as refined by Holmes and Brandeis in the Whitney case, that is to say, as a bar to substantive legislation restraining freedom of expression.

As has been indicated, this is not to say that clear and present danger afforded a clear-cut standard by which free speech claims could be determined in all cases. It has often been pointed out by certain members of the Court, as well as by commentators on its work, that the clear and present danger doctrine is nothing more than a brief way of characterizing an elaborate process of judgment, which involves balancing a complex variety of decision components, no one of which can be regarded as separately conclusive. To put it another way, clear and present danger, and indeed other tests, are but intellectual tools for appraising conflicting interests or values with which the Court is confronted.

The problem facing the Court in these cases is to reconcile the interest of the speaker and the community in the free expression of ideas with the protection of the public peace and of the primary uses of streets, parks, and other public facilities. In weighing the conflicting values involved in this process, a justice is necessarily guided by his conception of the judicial function and of the duties imposed upon him by the nature of this function. For example, Justice Frankfurter, with his strong attachment to the reasonable man theory would support the legislative judgment on the need for restraint unless it were clearly "unreasonable," whereas Justice Black would uphold the free speech claim unless the speech posed a clear, imminent, and serious danger to the public interest.

Although it is clearly impossible to isolate each of the values that each justice may have applied to the decision of a case, what happens in the determination of free speech cases of the kind examined in this chapter may be described as follows: The nature of the speech and the circumstances in which the utterance takes place are weighed or balanced against the need for restraint, the scope, method, and time of the restraint in relation to freedom of expression. To elaborate briefly on these factors, there are certain types of speech which have never been considered as entitled to constitutional protection because they effect injury without contributing anything to the process of rational discussion. These include the lewd and obscene, the libelous and the insulting or fighting words. Circumstances in which utterances take place may render otherwise innocent words dangerous and punishable. As Justice Holmes suggested in his famous Schenck opinion, it is one thing falsely to shout fire on a lonely hilltop, but it is quite another thing to shout fire in a crowded theater. Speech in the latter situation poses a threat of imminent and serious danger to the public safety. Speech that incites to crime is likewise beyond the pale of constitutional protection.

As to repressive regulation, it cannot be so broad in its scope or vague in its terms as to trap the innocent as well as the guilty. The law must prescribe for the guidance of administrators and courts reasonably clear and ascertainable standards of guilt and afford the citizen fair notice of what is forbidden. It makes a difference if a statute is narrowly drawn and directed to the specific evil aimed at or if it is drawn in such broad and vague terms as to encompass speech that is constitutionally protected.

Closely related to this problem is the question of the method by which freedom of expression is restrained in the public interest. This is well illustrated by the handbill cases previously considered. These cases do not hold that a community may not prevent the littering of its streets, but rather that the constitutional method of achieving this end is to punish those who litter the streets and not to ban all distribution of handbills.

Also, the time of impact of a restraining statute on speech is important. The position of previous restraint in our constitutional tradition is, of course, well known. The evil of previous restraint arises from the fact that it gags the speaker in advance, for fear that he will abuse freedom of speech if he is allowed to exercise it. This has generally been viewed by the Court as a very different matter from punishing speech that clearly and immediately threatens vital interests of the community. The weakness of prior restraint is that it deals with what may be rather than with what is or has been. In the 1940's the Court tended to condemn previous restraint on its face as a matter of course, but in the early 1950's the Court moved away from this on-its-face condemnation of previous restraint. The latter movement is reflected in the cases of *Breard* v. *Alexandria* and *Poulos* v. *New Hampshire* where prior restraint was upheld. Thus previous restraint is still viewed with a suspicious judicial eye, but it is no longer condemned out of hand.

THE HEYDAY OF CLEAR AND PRESENT DANGER

Despite the complex interplay of factors subsumed under the rubric "clear and present danger," and the consequent difficulty of appraising the relative weight given them in specific cases, it can be said that within the area and period of the cases reviewed here, the Court so interpreted the clear and present danger doctrine as to make of it the chief support of libertarian claims. Both the nature of the cases and the attitude of the Court operated to give clear and present danger a strong libertarian thrust in the decade preceding the "cold war." It was during these years that the test was clarified and reinforced by the theory of the preferred status of First Amendment freedoms. As thus strengthened, the clear and present danger test was employed by the Court to extend the protection of freedom of expression to include new situations such as picketing, criticism of judicial conduct, speech in public places by means of sound trucks, and motion pictures.

As previously noted, the cases here considered involved for the most part the conflict of the exercise of freedom of expression with the peace, good order, and convenience of the community as distinguished from the requirements of national security. Here, the Court has tended to sustain the claims of freedom in the absence of immediate and serious danger to the public interest.

Moreover, the majority of the justices of the Court in this period seemed to be fired with an evangelical zeal for libertarian values. This attitude can be illustrated by the following statement by Justice Black: "Freedom to speak and write about public questions is as important to the life of our government as is the heart to the human body. In fact, this privilege is the heart of our government. If that heart be weakened, the result is debilitation; if it be stilled, the result is death."[61]

Thus, the Court tended to place liberty above order in the absence of imminent and serious danger to other important interests of the community. This primacy of liberty over welfare and order found formal expression in the constitutional theory of preferred position of First Amendment freedoms. It was by application of this doctrine that the strongly libertarian justices defended an added emphasis on libertarian values.

Further analysis of the clear and present danger doctrine and its modification under "cold war" tensions will be reserved for Chapter 6.

[61] See his dissenting opinion in *Milk Wagon Drivers Union* v. *Meadowmoor Dairies,* 312 U.S. 287.

4   Freedom of Religion

FREE EXERCISE OF RELIGION

The victory for free exercise of religion signalized by the adoption of the First Amendment in 1791 was not seriously challenged in the first century and a half of our constitutional history, and hence there was little occasion for the Supreme Court to intervene in defense of the freedom formalized in 1791.

It was, of course, well known that the clause in the First Amendment that "Congress shall make no law . . . prohibiting the free exercise" of religion limited only federal action and did not apply to state restrictions of First Amendment freedoms.[1] Indeed, it was long thought that the due process clause of the Fourteenth Amendment imposed no such limitations upon state action. As indicated in Chapter 2, the Supreme Court in 1922 declared that "neither the Fourteenth Amendment nor any other provision of the Constitution imposes restrictions upon the state about freedom of speech."[2] The logic of this declaration, of course, applies to freedom of religion and other First Amendment freedoms. Thus, the Supreme Court could exercise its jurisdiction to safeguard a claimed violation of religious freedom only if the violation was committed by an agency of the federal government.

Federal Restraints

The decisions of the Supreme Court involving Congressional power over religious freedom, as limited by the free exercise clause of the First Amendment, have concerned, for the most part, laws relating to the practice or advocacy of polygamy as a doctrine of the Mormon Church and conscientious objection to

---

[1] *Permoli* v. *New Orleans,* 44 U.S. 589, 609 (1845).
[2] *Prudential Life Insurance Co.* v. *Cheek,* 259 U.S. 530 (1922).

military service.[3] It was in these cases that the Court first delineated in broad strokes the nature and scope of the *free exercise* right.

In its first consideration of this right, the Court sustained a federal statute forbidding bigamy as a crime in the Territory of Utah. To the plea of the defendant that the act denied him the free exercise of his religious beliefs as a Mormon, the Court answered that although "Congress was deprived of all legislative power over mere opinion," it was left "free to reach actions which were in violation of social duties or subversive of good order."[4] Religious belief could not be pleaded against an overt act made criminal by the law of the land. Laws may not interfere with religious beliefs or opinions, but they may interfere with religious practices. To allow conduct in violation of law to be excused on the ground of religious belief "would be to make the professed doctrines of religious belief superior to the law of the land, and in effect to permit every citizen to become a law unto himself."[5]

It was the purpose of the free exercise clause of the First Amendment to allow everyone under the jurisdiction of the United States to hold such beliefs respecting his relation to the Deity and his obligations thereunder as meet the approval of his judgment and conscience and to express his beliefs in such form as he may think proper, so long as there is no injury to the rights of others.[6] This includes the right to teach and propagate any religious doctrine "which does not violate the laws of morality and property and does not infringe personal rights."[7]

Nor can religious belief be cited to obtain exemption from legally imposed obligations of general application, such as military service. Thus there is no constitutional right which relieves conscientious objectors from military service.[8] Nevertheless, Congress may as an act of grace grant such immunity. In 1918 the Court

[3] *Hamilton* v. *Regents,* 293 U.S. 245 (1934) and *Arver* v. *United States* 245 U.S. 366 (1918).

[4] *Reynolds* v. *United States,* 98 U.S. 145 (1878).

[5] *Ibid.,* 167.

[6] *Davis* v. *Beason,* 133 Wall. 333 (1890) and *Watson* v. *Jones,* 13 Wall. 679 (1871).

[7] *Ibid.*

[8] *Hamilton* v. *Regents,* 293 U.S. 245 (1934).

summarily rejected, as completely unsound, the argument that the Selective Service Act was repugnant to the religious freedom clause of the First Amendment because of the exemption granted to ministers of religion, theological students, and members of sects whose beliefs deny the moral right to engage in war.[9]

In a series of cases,[10] starting in 1929 the Court on three successive occasions first construed the Naturalization Act so as to deny the privilege of naturalization to those who, because of religious belief or other conscientious scruples, refused to promise to bear arms in defense of the United States. Yet, in *Girouard* v. *United States*,[11] in 1946, these decisions were overruled, and the Court held that conscientious objection to bearing arms did not constitute a lack of attachment to the United States. In admitting Girouard to citizenship, the Court stated that it was unwilling to assume that Congress in passing the Naturalization Act had intended to repudiate our long-standing tradition of religious liberty by barring from citizenship those who conscientiously objected to military service on religious grounds. The language of the oath did not require that interpretation. This decision was reaffirmed and extended in *Colmstaedt* v. *Immigration and Naturalization Service*,[12] where refusal on religious grounds to participate in the production of munitions or to deliver them to combat troops did not disqualify an applicant for naturalization.

Of course, it is not to be inferred from the last two cases that Congress is without constitutional power to make religiously inspired pacifism a barrier to citizenship. On the contrary, Congress has complete power to grant or withhold the privilege of naturalization on any grounds, or for no reason at all, that it sees fit.

These doctrines have been reaffirmed and sharpened in a more recent case involving state action. In *Cantwell* v. *Connecticut,* the Court declared that freedom of conscience and freedom to adhere to such forms of worship as the individual may choose cannot be restricted by law. But the state will protect him in the exercise of his chosen form of religion. "Thus the Amendment

[9] *Arver* v. *United States* 245 U.S. 366 (1918).

[10] *United States* v. *Schwimmer,* 279 U.S. 644 (1929); *United States* v. *MacIntosh,* 283 U.S. 605 (1931); *United States* v. *Bland,* 283 U.S. 636 (1931).

[11] 328 U.S. 61 (1946).   [12] 339 U.S. 901 (1950).

embraces two concepts—freedom to believe and freedom to act. The first is absolute, but in the nature of things, the second cannot be."[13]

In the language of the cases, the rule for the guidance of Congressional action may be summarized as follows: One has the right to practice any religious principle and to teach any religious doctrine which does not violate the laws established by society for the good order and morality of the community, and which does not restrict or injure the personal rights of others.

State and Local Restraints

It was, of course, not until after it had been determined that the specific inhibitions of the First Amendment were applicable to the states through the due process clause of the Fourteenth Amendment that the Supreme Court became the guardian of religious liberty against the states. Since 1937, nearly all religious freedom cases have arisen from state rather than federal action. Indeed, it was not until after the Supreme Court had made this important determination that there reached the Court a sufficient number of cases from which there could be developed a constitutional law of religious freedom in any substantial sense. Thus, it is not an exaggeration to say that the constitutional law of religious freedom, for the most part, has evolved out of court decisions since the middle 1930's. Obviously, the incorporation of religious freedom into the "liberty" protected by the Fourteenth Amendment against state deprivation was an inseparable part of the significant evolution that brought the other First Amendment freedoms within the scope of the concept. Because of the relatively limited area for federal restrictions on religious freedom, it may be said that the relevant clause of the First Amendment has found its chief value through incorporation into the Fourteenth Amendment.[14]

The decision of the Supreme Court to review state restrictions on religious freedom brought forth a veritable rash of cases by a small but aggressive religious sect, known as Jehovah's Witnesses.

[13] 310 U.S. 296, 303, 304 (1940).
[14] See Leo Pfeffer, "The Supreme Court as Protector of Civil Rights: Freedom of Religion," *The Annals,* Vol. 275 (May, 1951), p. 76.

A summary of these and other cases involving state encroachment on the free exercise of religion follows. Although the Fourteenth Amendment had been a part of the Constitution for nearly three quarters of a century, it was not until 1940 that the Supreme Court handed down the first decision squarely holding that the religious freedom embraced in the First Amendment is equally protected against state action by the due process clause of the Fourteenth Amendment. To be sure, several earlier Witness cases [15] had established the right to distribute religious literature on the streets and in public places without prior permission of any public officer, but these cases were decided under freedom of speech and press guarantees, without consideration of freedom of religion.

In *Cantwell* v. *Connecticut*,[16] decided in May, 1940, the Court specifically declared for the first time that the concept of liberty embodied in the Fourteenth Amendment embraces the religious liberties guaranteed by the First Amendment and renders the legislatures of the states as incompetent as Congress to enact the forbidden laws. Here, three Witnesses were convicted for violating a state statute requiring that, before persons might solicit money for religious or charitable causes, they must first apply to the secretary of the local public welfare council. He was to determine whether the cause was a religious one or bona fide object of charity or philanthropy, and on this basis issue his certificate of authorization. The Court held the statute, as applied to the Witnesses, an unconstitutional deprivation of religious freedom in violation of the Fourteenth Amendment. Justice Roberts, speaking for a unanimous Court, declared:[17]

. . . to condition the solicitation of aid for the perpetuation of religious views or systems upon a license, the grant of which rests in the exercise of a determination by state authority as to what is a religious cause, is to lay a forbidden burden upon the exercise of liberty protected by the Constitution.

The Court was careful to point out that nothing said in the opinion "is intended even remotely to imply that under the cloak of religion, persons may, with impunity, commit frauds upon the

---

[15] For example, *Lovell* v. *Griffin*, 303 U.S. 444 (1938), and *Schneider* v. *Irvington*, 308 U.S. 147 (1939).

[16] 310 U.S. 296.   [17] *Ibid.*, p. 300.

public."[18] A state may undoubtedly protect its citizens from fraudulent solicitation by requiring a stranger in the community, as a condition of publicly soliciting funds for any purpose, to establish his identity and his authority to act for the cause which he allegedly represents. But the method here adopted by Connecticut to that end violates the liberty safeguarded by the Fourteenth Amendment.

The Court also reversed the conviction of one of the Cantwells on a common law charge of inciting a breach of the peace in the playing of phonograph records which were offensive to his Catholic auditors. The Court held that in the absence of a statute narrowly drawn to define and punish specific conduct as constituting a clear and present danger to a substantial interest of the state, Cantwell's record playing, considered in the light of constitutional guarantees, raised no such clear and present menace to public peace as to render him liable to conviction for the common law offense in question.

From now on, the somewhat erratic course of judicial decision in the field of religious freedom is evidence of the difficulty encountered by the Court in fashioning reliable criteria for the proper balancing of the right to free exercise of religion against the social interest of the community as expressed through the police power.

Since many of the cases pertinent to the subject of this chapter involve a merging of issues of free press with issues of religious freedom, and have therefore been analyzed in the preceding chapter, they will not be further considered here, but the consequences for religious freedom will be summarized later. These cases, it will be remembered, include those involving the requirement of official permits or licenses for the distribution of religious literature, and for the solicitation of funds for religious purposes, as well as those involving the regulation of religious speech in public places.

Perhaps the stormiest controversy stirred up by Jehovah's Witnesses resulted from their defiance of the compulsory flag salute statutes. Within two weeks after the Cantwell decision, the

[18] *Ibid.*

Supreme Court, in the widely criticized Gobitis case,[19] held that freedom of religion was not violated by a state law requiring expulsion from the public schools of pupils who on grounds of religious scruples refused to salute the flag of the United States.

Mr. Justice Frankfurter, speaking for an 8 to 1 majority, stated the issue of the case in the following language:[20]

"We live by symbols." The flag is the symbol of our national unity, transcending all internal differences, however large, within the framework of the Constitution. . . . The precise issue . . . is whether the legislatures of the various states and the authorities in a thousand counties and school districts of this country are barred from determining the appropriateness of various means to evoke that unifying sentiment without which there can be ultimately no liberties, civil or religious. . . .

So to hold would make us in effect the school board of the country. That authority has not been given to this Court, nor should we assume it.

Aside from his oratorical tribute to flag salute symbolism, what Justice Frankfurter seems to be saying here is that the flag salute statute raises a political question which must be determined by public opinion and not by the judiciary.

Justice Stone's solitary but vigorous dissent stated clearly his conception of the relationship of the constitutional guarantee of religious liberty and the problem of majority versus minority rights. He pointed out that by this law the state seeks to coerce these children "to express a sentiment which, as they interpret it, they do not entertain, and which violates their deepest religious convictions."[21] In reply to Frankfurter's doctrine of judicial abstention, Justice Stone asserted:[22]

I am not persuaded that we should refrain from passing upon the legislative judgment "as long as the remedial channels of the democratic process remain open and unobstructed." This seems to me no less than the surrender of the constitutional protection of the liberty of small minorities to the popular will. . . . Here we have such a small minority entertaining in good faith a religious belief which is such a departure from the usual course of human conduct that most persons are disposed

[19] *Minersville School District* v. *Gobitis,* 310 U.S. 586 (1940).
[20] *Ibid.,* 598.
[21] *Ibid.*
[22] *Ibid.,* 603, 604.

to regard it with little toleration or concern. In such circumstances careful scrutiny of legislative efforts to secure conformity of belief and opinion by a compulsory affirmation of the desired belief is especially needful if civil rights are to receive any protection.

The increase of mob violence toward the Witnesses after this decision gave melancholy support to Mr. Justice Stone's dissent. Ironically enough, the flag, intended as a symbol of freedom, had become for many persons an instrument of oppression of a religious minority. It was misused to deny the very freedoms it was intended to symbolize.[23]

In *West Virginia State Board of Education* v. *Barnette*,[24] in 1943, the Supreme Court specifically overruled the Gobitis case. Inspired by the Gobitis ruling, the West Virginia State Board of Education (under permissive state law) adopted a resolution requiring all students and teachers to salute and pledge allegiance to the flag as a routine part of the daily school program. Speaking by Justice Jackson, the Court in a 6 to 3 decision held that "the action of the local authorities in compelling the flag salute and pledge transcends constitutional limitations on their power and involves the sphere of intellect and spirit which it is the purpose of the First Amendment . . . to reserve from all official control. . . ." Striking with even greater force than had Justice Stone at Frankfurter's judicial self-restraint doctrine in such cases, Jackson declared:

The very purpose of a Bill of Rights was to withdraw certain subjects from the vicissitudes of political controversy, to place them beyond the reach of majorities and officials and to establish them as legal principles to be applied by the courts. One's right to life, liberty and property, to free speech, a free press, freedom of worship and assembly, and other fundamental rights may not be submitted to vote; they depend on the outcome of no elections.

Invoking the clear and present danger test, Jackson pointed out that state restriction of these fundamental freedoms may not be judged by the same due process standard as, for example, the regulation of a public utility. "They are susceptible of restriction

[23] For a statement of facts relative to this situation, see Victor Rotnem **and** F. G. Folsome, Jr., "Recent Restrictions upon Religious Liberty," *American Political Science Review*, Vol. 36 (December, 1952), pp. 1161–1163.
[24] 319 U.S. 624 (1943).

only to prevent grave and immediate danger to interests which the state may lawfully protect." Further, the history of coercive uniformity shows that those who begin with the elimination of dissent end with the elimination of dissenters. Finally, "If there is any fixed star in our constitutional constellation, it is that no official, high or petty, can prescribe what shall be orthodox in politics, nationalism, religion or other matters of opinion or force citizens to confess by word or act their faith therein."

In *Taylor* v. *Mississippi*,[25] decided on the same day as the Barnette case, the Court added a corollary to the Barnette principle by holding invalid a Mississippi statute which made it unlawful to urge people, on religious grounds, not to salute the flag. The Court reasoned that if the state may not constrain one to violate his conscientious religious tenets by saluting the flag, it may not by the same token punish him for publicly communicating his views on the subject to his fellows and exhorting them to accept those views.

Restrictions on Religious Speech in Public Places

Two later decisions consider state restrictions against speaking on religious subjects in public parks without permits from public authorities. In *Niemotko* v. *Maryland*,[26] members of Jehovah's Witnesses had been found guilty of disorderly conduct because of their attempt to hold a meeting in a town park without a permit. There was actually no evidence of disorderly conduct on the part of the Witnesses. They had already applied for and been refused a permit by local officials, acting not under statutory authorization but in accordance with a local custom under which permits had been issued to other religious and fraternal organizations. In response to their application for permits, the Witnesses were questioned concerning their religious beliefs rather than on matters related to the orderly use of the park. The Supreme Court in reversing the conviction concluded that the Witnesses had been denied the use of the park because of the officials' dislike of them or their religious views and that such discrimination was a denial of the equal protection of the laws.

[25] 319 U.S. 583 (1943).
[26] 340 U.S. 268 (1951).

In *Kunz* v. *New York*,[27] decided on the same day as Niemotko, the conviction of a Baptist minister for conducting religious services in the streets of New York City, without a license from the police commissioner, as required by a city ordinance, was reversed by the Supreme Court. Kunz had been refused a license after a hearing, presumably because he had in the past ridiculed and denounced other religious beliefs in offensive and provocative language and thereby created a condition of strife and threatened violence in violation of the aforementioned ordinance. The Supreme Court reversed the conviction since the ordinance vested an unrestrained discretion in the police commissioner to grant or not to grant a permit with no appropriate standards to guide his action.

Justice Jackson, in dissent, agreed with the New York Court of Appeals "that when, as here, the applicant, claims a constitutional right to incite riots, and a constitutional right to the services of policemen to quell those riots, then a permit need not be issued."

In a still more recent case, the Court invalidated a New York statute because in the judgment of the Court it interfered with the right of a church to choose its own hierarchy of officials and to administer its own property. Such a right has constitutional protection "as a part of the free exercise of religion against state interference."[28]

Cases Lost by Religious Sects

It must not be assumed from the foregoing that the police power of the states has suffered complete defeat at the hands of freedom of religion. The Witnesses and other religious sects have lost a number of cases. For example, the Court has sustained a state statute forbidding a parade or procession upon a public street without a license, against the contention of the defendants that the procession was a form of worship and interference therewith violated the due process clause of the Fourteenth Amendment. The parade here involved the marching of Jehovah's Witnesses, in groups of 15 to 25 members each, in close single file, along the sidewalks of the business district of a densely populated city.

[27] 340 U.S. 290 (1951).
[28] *Kedroff* v. *St. Nicholas Cathedral,* 344 U.S. 94 (1952).

The Court, speaking through Chief Justice Hughes, noted that the authority of a municipality to regulate public highways in order to assure the safety and convenience of the people has never been regarded as inconsistent with civil liberties, but rather as one of the means of safeguarding the good order of the community upon which civil liberties ultimately depend. "Civil liberties, as guaranteed by the Constitution, imply the existence of an organized society maintaining public order without which liberty itself would be lost in the excesses of unrestrained abuses."[29]

The question in a case of this kind is whether the regulation of the use of the streets is exercised in such a manner as not to deny or unwarrantably curtail the important rights of assembly and communication traditionally associated with resort to public places.

The Witnesses suffered another setback in *Chaplinsky* v. *New Hampshire*.[30] Here the Court again unanimously decided that a state statute, which forbade anyone to address "any offensive, derisive or annoying word to any other person who is lawfully in any street or other public place" or to ". . . call him by any offensive or derisive name," had been validly applied to the conduct of a Jehovah's Witness. To a city marshal who had warned him against inciting a public disturbance, Chaplinsky addressed the epithets: "God damned racketeer" and "damned Fascist." This language was defended as an exercise of religious freedom, but Mr. Justice Murphy, himself no mean champion of religious freedom, declared, for the Court, that he "could not conceive that cursing a public officer is the exercise of religion in any sense of the term." The prevention and punishment of certain well-defined and narrowly limited categories of speech have always been regarded as outside the sphere of constitutional protection. These include the insulting or "fighting" words, "which by their very utterance inflict injury, or tend to incite immediate breach of the peace." Such words "are no essential part of any exposition of ideas and are of such slight social value as a step to truth that any benefit that may be derived from them is clearly outweighed by the social interest in order and morality."

In 1944, the Court sustained a provision of a Massachusetts

[29] *Cox* v. *New Hampshire,* 312 U.S. 569 (1941).
[30] 315 U.S. 568 (1942).

child labor statute, making it unlawful for children to sell newspapers or periodicals on the streets or in other public places, and for a parent or guardian to permit a child to work in violation of this prohibition. In *Prince* v. *Massachusetts*, the statute was applied against one Sarah Prince, a member of the Witnesses, who had her nine-year-old niece accompany her in the distribution of religious literature on the public streets. Mr. Justice Rutledge held for the Court that the statute as applied here was a valid exercise of the state police power, since "Democratic society depends for its continuance upon the healthy well-rounded growth of young people into full maturity as citizens with all that implies," and "to this end it may take appropriate steps against the crippling effects of child employment."[31] These are noble words, but the question arises whether they pertain to the facts of this case. It may be doubted that the work in which this child was engaged in the company of her aunt constituted a danger to the protected social interest of sufficient seriousness to justify such interference with her religious freedom.

Justice Jackson, in a forceful dissent, in which he was joined by Justices Roberts and Frankfurter, maintained that the limits on religious activities "begin to operate whenever activities begin to affect or collide with the liberties of others or of the public. Religious activities which concern only members of the faith . . . ought to be as nearly absolutely free as anything can be." But when a religious group enters the secular market, it is then participating in "Caesar's affairs and may be regulated by the state" provided that such regulation is not arbitrary and does not discriminate against anyone because of his religious purpose.[32]

In 1949, the Supreme Court, for want of a substantial federal question, dismissed a case in which a church group contended that religious freedom was violated by a zoning ordinance forbidding the building of churches in certain residential areas.[33]

[31] *Prince* v. *Massachusetts*, 321 U.S. 158 (1944).

[32] For a lucid analysis of Jackson's opinions on this and other First Amendment freedoms, see Robert J. Steamer, "Mr. Justice Jackson and the First Amendment," *University of Pittsburgh Law Review*, Vol. 15 (Winter, 1954), pp. 193–221.

[33] *Corporation of the Presiding Bishop of the Church of Jesus Christ of Latter-Day Saints* v. *City of Porterville*, 338 U.S. 805 (1949).

An interesting and somewhat puzzling case, merging free speech and freedom of religion, was decided in 1953. In *Poulos v. New Hampshire*,[34] the Supreme Court of the United States sustained the conviction of a Jehovah's Witness for holding a religious meeting in a public park without a license from the City Council as required by ordinance, although the defendant had been arbitrarily and illegally refused a permit by the Council in response to his efforts to comply with the requirements of the ordinance. The State Supreme Court had held that the ordinance was valid, on the authority of *Cox* v. *New Hampshire*, but that it must be administered fairly and without discrimination, and that in the instant case the Council had arbitrarily and illegally denied the license. However, Poulos should not have violated the ordinance but should have sought relief from illegal refusal through review by certiorari, as prescribed by state law.

The Supreme Court of the United States, sustaining the conviction, declared through Justice Reed that since the ordinance must be administered fairly, it was only a routine police measure and involved no previous restraint on liberty of speech or religion.

This case presents the curious, but not unique, phenomenon of the Court's formally adhering to libertarian principles but arriving at antilibertarian results. To say that Poulos did not suffer restraint of religious freedom is to use words without substance. The Court, in brief, held that one may be constitutionally punished for holding a religious meeting without a license, which has been arbitrarily and illegally refused by those responsible for administering the ordinance requiring it. Justice Reed admitted that the delay and expense incident to judicial review of an arbitrary refusal of a license is unfortunate, "but the expense and annoyance of litigation is a price citizens must pay for life in an orderly society." This argument comes perilously close to implying the absurd proposition that freedom of speech and religion are guaranteed only to those who have the patience to wait and the money to pay.

It may well be, as Justice Reed argued, that to allow a person to proceed to hold a public meeting in a city park without prior arrangement is to invite breaches of the peace or create public

[34] 345 U.S. 395 (1953).

dangers, but this ignores the fact that Poulos had in good faith sought to make the necessary arrangements and in the face of this was illegally refused a permit. Justice Black, in dissent, mourned this as one of a series of recent decisions "which fail to protect the rights of Americans to speak freely."

SUMMARY ANALYSIS OF JUDICIAL CRITERIA OF RELIGIOUS FREEDOM CASES

It would be difficult to draw, from the preceding cases, a definite pattern of the constitutional law of religious freedom that would have dependable predictive value. Nevertheless, there are certain criteria of judicial judgment which have been applied in most of the cases. These may be briefly stated: On the side of doctrine, it may be said that the same principles apply to freedom of religion as to other First Amendment freedoms. Thus the clear and present danger test applies equally to all these freedoms. An interference with religious freedom, then, is constitutionally justifiable only when clearly and immediately necessary to protect a more important social interest than the unrestrained exercise of religion. This necessarily involves the exercise of value judgments on the relative importance of the unrestrained exercise of religion and the social interest threatened thereby, the imminence and clarity of the danger occasioned by the free exercise of religion, and whether the danger can be averted without invasion of the constitutional right. In each of these situations, judgment is exercised in the light of the preferred position accorded the freedoms protected by the First Amendment, and the presumption is against the validity of the restriction which means that the burden of proof is on the government to establish validity. Although there are exceptions to the explicit application of these principles, they are implicit in nearly all the religious freedom cases.[35]

Nevertheless, whatever judicial canons are employed by the Court in rationalizing its conclusions and whatever the diversity of opinion with respect to their applicability, it is apparent in all these cases that the justices are weighing the right to religious freedom against the interest of the community threatened by the exercise of the claimed right and are determining which, in the circum-

[35] Pfeffer, *op. cit.*, p. 78.

stances, is the more important interest. The criteria most generally and frequently selected to aid this balancing process are those set forth previously, namely, clear and present danger reinforced by the theory of preferred status.

The preceding pages afford numerous examples of the application of these criteria. Only a few need be recalled here: The Court in the first Mormon case unanimously determined that the interest of the community in monogamous marriage outweighed the right of the Mormons to practice their religious belief in polygamous marriage and that such a danger to the community could be effectively averted only by forbidden plural marriages. The state's paramount interest in maintaining order and in preventing abuse to innocent persons overrides the right of a Jehovah's Witness to curse and vilify a city official in the public streets. On the other hand, the community's interest in maintaining unlittered streets may not be effected by forbidding the distribution of religious handbills. Nor may the state's interest in safeguarding enjoyment of the privacy of the home override the right of religious proselyters to ring door bells in order to offer the occupants religious pamphlets. Likewise, the state's interest in preventing fraud may not be protected by the granting of unbridled discretion to a public official to withhold the right of soliciting religious contributions from anyone not adjudged by him as representing a bona fide religious cause. Nor may the state's legitimate interest in promoting patriotism be effected by compelling school children to salute the flag in violation of their religious scruples.

In none of these cases, then, did the Court question the right of the state to protect the interest involved; it simply held that infringement of religious liberty was neither a valid nor a necessary means of achieving the desired end.

It should be added, as previously noted, that the members of the Court have not always been in agreement on the applicability of these criteria of judicial judgment. The diversity expresses itself (1) as between different justices in the same cases, (2) in the position of the Court from case to case, and (3) in the position of the same justice in different cases. Illustrative of the first point is the partial dissent from the prevailing position of the Court by Justice Jackson and the apparently complete dissent of Justice

Frankfurter. Jackson's position—which, as will be seen, should be termed his later position—was set forth in his dissenting opinion in the Prince case, where he made it clear that he would confine the application of the foregoing criteria of judgment to religious activities that concern only members of the faith. When a religious group goes outside its own ranks and enters the secular market, it is then participating in "Caesar's affairs and may be regulated by the state," subject only to the regular due process limitation of reasonableness.[36]

In Frankfurter's view, no constitutional rights are entitled to a preferred status. Hence, religious freedom is due no greater judicial protection than ordinary commercial interests, and legislation restricting such freedom must be sustained or invalidated on the basis of the presence or absence of rational justification.[37]

The shift in the position of the Court from case to case is sharply illustrated by the two flag salute cases, in the first of which Frankfurter's passion for judicial self-restraint prevailed by 8 to 1, whereas in the second Jackson rested the decision of the Court squarely on the doctrines of clear and present danger and preferred status.

The shift in the position of the same justice from case to case also finds an exemplar in Justice Jackson, who in the second flag salute case took a position which stamped him as one of the most vigorous defenders of the clear and present danger test and related criteria; later, in the Prince case, he apparently had become convinced that the Court went too far in sustaining the religious excesses of Jehovah's Witnesses.

SUMMARY OF HOLDINGS ON FREE EXERCISE OF RELIGION

From the cases discussed here, the following rights and limitations seem to have been established: A person may distribute religious literature on the streets and in other public places without prior permission from any public official;[38] he may even

[36] 321 U.S. 158 (1944).

[37] See his dissent in *West Virginia State Board of Education* v. *Barnette,* 319 U.S. 624 (1943).

[38] *Lovell* v. *Griffin,* 303 U.S. 444; *Schneider* v. *Irvington,* 308 U.S. 149; *Largent* v. *Texas,* 318 U.S. 418.

circulate religious literature in a privately owned town[39] and in a federally owned housing project[40] without the permission of the owners; he may play phonograph records to any willing listener on the streets for purposes of religious propaganda,[41] and he may ring door bells in the same cause;[42] he may sell religious literature or solicit funds for a religious cause without a permit or payment of a license tax,[43] and he may do this even if he makes his living entirely from the sale of religious books.[44]

It is unconstitutional for a state or one of its agencies of local government to require pupils in the public schools to salute the flag and to give a pledge of allegiance contrary to the religious scruples of the pupils.[45] Nor can one be punished for publicly urging others not to salute the flag.[46]

Under the naturalization laws, refusal to bear arms in defense of country in wartime is no bar to the grant of citizenship to a conscientious objector willing to perform noncombatant service.[47]

In connection with the holding of religious meetings in public parks, no religious sect may be discriminated against because of its religious beliefs.[48] Nor may a state vest unrestrained discretion in a police officer to grant or not to grant a permit to speak on religious subjects in a public park; furthermore, a minister who has been denied a permit under such conditions may not be punished for preaching without a permit even though he may have ridiculed and denounced other religious beliefs.[49]

The right of a church to choose its own official hierarchy and to administer its own property is entitled to constitutional protection against state interference.[50]

[39] *Marsh* v. *Alabama,* 326 U.S. 501 (1946).
[40] *Tucker* v. *Texas,* 326 U.S. 517 (1946).
[41] *Cantwell* v. *Connecticut,* 310 U.S. 296 (1940).
[42] *Martin* v. *Struthers,* 319 U.S. 141 (1943).
[43] *Murdock* v. *Pennsylvania,* 319 U.S. 105 (1943).
[44] *Follet* v. *McCormick,* 321 U.S. 573 (1944).
[45] *West Virginia State Board of Education* v. *Barnette,* 319 U.S. 624 (1943), overruling *Minersville School District* v. *Gobitis,* 310 U.S. 586 (1940).
[46] *Taylor* v. *Mississippi,* 319 U.S. 583 (1943).
[47] *Girouard* v. *United States,* 328 U.S. 61 (1946).
[48] *Niemotko* v. *Maryland,* 340 U.S. 268 (1951).
[49] *Kunz* v. *New York,* 340 U.S. 290 (1951).
[50] *Kedroff* v. *St. Nicholas Cathedral,* 344 U.S. 94 (1952).

The following restrictions on the exercise of religion have been upheld by the Court: The practice of polygamy may be forbidden without violation of the constitutional right to freedom of religion.[51] A city ordinance regulating the use of streets for religious parades and processions and imposing a reasonable nondiscriminatory fee for the cost of administration is valid.[52] So also is a state statute forbidding and punishing the addressing of offensive and derisive language to anyone who is lawfully in any street or other public place.[53] Moreover, state child labor laws may validly be applied to those who permit children under their care to sell religious literature on the streets.[54] A state may require male students enrolled in the state university to take a course in military training as one of the conditions of attendance, without exempting conscientious and religious objectors to military training from the requirement.[55] The Court has even sustained state exclusion of a conscientious objector from the practice of law.[56]

Finally, a person may be constitutionally punished for holding a religious meeting in a public park without a permit as required by ordinance, even though he has properly sought the permit and been arbitrarily and illegally refused by those responsible for administering the ordinance, if the state provides a judicial remedy for such arbitrary refusal.[57]

THE ESTABLISHMENT CLAUSE

The rest of this chapter will consider the Court's interpretation of the clause of the First Amendment forbidding Congress to make any "law respecting an establishment of religion," which like the free exercise clause has been held applicable to the states through the due process clause of the Fourteenth Amendment.

Before 1947 the interpretations of this clause had given the Court little difficulty. Unlike free exercise of religion, the establishment clause was almost untested so far as the Supreme Court was

[51] *Reynolds* v. *United States,* 98 U.S. 145 (1878).
[52] *Cox* v. *New Hampshire,* 312 U.S. 569 (1941).
[53] *Chaplinsky* v. *New Hampshire,* 315 U.S. 568 (1942).
[54] *Prince* v. *Massachusetts,* 321 U.S. 158 (1944).
[55] *Hamilton* v. *Regents,* 293 U.S. 245 (1934).
[56] In re *Summers,* 325 U.S. 561 (1945).
[57] *Poulos* v. *New Hampshire,* 345 U.S. 395 (1953).

concerned. Indeed, there had been only four cases[58] before the Court in more than a century and a half, when in 1947 it was suddenly confronted with the highly sensitive and controversial issue of public aid to private, sectarian schools. The task of the Court today is complicated not only by the absence of applicable judicial precedents, but also by the fact that the intentions of the framers of the establishment clause have been obscured by the passage of time, and that diverse attitudes and traditions have arisen to confuse the accepted meaning of the clause, if such can be said to exist. Even more important is the fact that the modern application of the clause involves situations which were unknown to the framers and could not have been foreseen by them.[59]

It is true, of course, that in 1930 the use of public funds to purchase secular textbooks for pupils in parochial schools in Louisiana was sustained.[60] But here the establishment clause was not considered because the action of Louisiana was contested on the ground that it violated the due process clause of the Fourteenth Amendment by spending tax funds for a private purpose. The Court reasoned that since the tax funds were used for the benefit of the children and not for the sectarian schools, the appropriation was for a public purpose, and the fact that the schools were operated by members of a particular sect did not alter the character of the appropriation. It is apparent, then, that up to this time virtually nothing had been done by the Supreme Court to fix the boundaries of the establishment clause. Starting in 1947, the Court decided three important cases which contributed little to illuminating the meaning of the establishment clause, if, indeed, they did not further obscure it.

Wall of Separation Doctrine

In *Everson* v. *Board of Education*,[61] the Supreme Court encountered a new problem. The question presented was the validity

[58] *Bradfield* v. *Roberts*, 175 U.S. 291 (1899); *Quick Bear* v. *Leup*, 210 U.S. 50 (1908); *Cochran* v. *Louisiana State Board*, 281 U.S. 370 (1930); Selective Draft Law cases, 245 U.S. 366 (1918).

[59] For a good discussion of these matters, see L. A. Lardner, "How Far Does the Constitution Separate Church and State," *American Political Science Review*, Vol. 45 (March, 1951), pp. 110–132.

[60] *Cochran* v. *Louisiana State Board*, 281 U.S. 370 (1930).

[61] 330 U.S. 1 (1947).

of a New Jersey statute authorizing the payment from tax-raised funds of the bus fares of Catholic parochial school pupils, as part of a program of paying the cost of transporting all pupils attending "schools other than private schools operated for profit." The holding of the Court sustaining these expenditures for the cost of transporting children to sectarian schools seems clearly inconsistent with its construction of the establishment clause in the same case.

At the outset the Court made it clear for the first time that the establishment clause, as well as the free exercise clause, of the First Amendment is made applicable to the states by the Fourteenth Amendment.

Also for the first time, the Court sought to give meaning to the establishment clause in these words:

> The "establishment of religion" clause of the First Amendment means at least this: Neither a state nor the Federal Government can set up a church. Neither can pass laws which aid one religion, aid all religions, or prefer one religion over another. Neither can force nor influence a person to go to or to remain away from church against his will or force him to profess a belief or disbelief in any religion. No person can be punished for entertaining or professing religious beliefs or disbeliefs, for church attendance or non-attendance. No tax in any amount, large or small, can be levied to support any religious activities or institutions, whatever they may be called, or whatever form they may adopt to teach or practice religion. Neither a state nor the Federal Government can, openly or secretly, participate in the affairs of any religious organization or groups and *vice versa*. In the words of Jefferson, the clause against the establishment of religion by law was intended to erect "a wall of separation between church and state."

Coming then to the specific issue before it, the Court insisted that the New Jersey legislation does no more than provide a general program to help parents get their children, regardless of their religion, safely and expeditiously to and from accredited schools. In short, this is a welfare program in aid of the pupils and not in support of the church schools. These payments, then, were sustained by the Court majority of 5 only because they were deemed in aid of the children and not in aid of the sectarian schools. This, declared Mr. Justice Black for the majority, "does not breach the wall of separation between church and state."

The majority, however, seems to have overlooked the fact, as Mr. Justice Jackson so forcefully pointed out in dissent, that the beneficiaries of these bus fare payments were selected by an essentially religious test. Before making payments to reimburse parents for pupils' bus fares, the school authorities must ask whether the school attended is a Catholic school, and if it is not, the aid is not afforded.

Moreover, the conclusion of the Court was reached in the face of its unequivocal declaration that "New Jersey cannot consistently with the 'establishment of religion' clause . . . contribute funds to the support of an institution which teaches the tenets and faith of any church." It is difficult to see how the grant of public funds to pay transportation costs of children to and from parochial schools, whose major objective is the teaching of sectarian doctrine, can be squared with this declaration. If the sectarian purposes of the school are aided by payment of bus fares, in that it helps to get children to the school who might not otherwise go there, as the Court majority conceded; if, as is presumed, a direct appropriation to the school would be invalid, is not an indirect appropriation equally invalid? The difference would seem to be in name and method, not in substance.

Furthermore, it might be asked, where does this welfare theory end? If the purchase of textbooks and the payment of bus fares for the pupils of parochial schools are constitutional, what is unconstitutional, other than distinctly sectarian services and supplies? How far can the state go in aiding church schools in the name of promoting the public welfare, with incidental sectarian benefits? May it supply the pupils of those schools with such nonsectarian aids as free lunches, free school clinics, free blackboards, free notebooks, free pencils, and salaries for teachers of nonsectarian subjects? Clearly, the Everson case raises more questions than it answers.

On the other hand, some of the limitations stated by Justice Black as required by the establishment clause of the First Amendment seem to be extreme, as well as inconsistent with the Court's holding in the case. For example, when he says that the First Amendment means at least this: "Neither a state nor the Federal Government . . . can pass laws which aid . . . all religions," some troublesome questions arise. The extension of tax exemption to church property and to gifts made to churches or religious causes is surely aid to religion. Can it be that these practices are invalid? The Court seems to assume that they are not, but the question is an open one.

And Justice Black assures us that all this was done without making the slightest breach in the wall separating church and state. Four of his fellow justices were less complacent about the Court's holdings, as were many outside the Court. Indeed, the most obvious result of the Everson decision was to stir up the very sort of bitter religious controversy which the original supporters of the First Amendment had sought to prevent.

A year after the Everson case, the Court in *McCollum* v. *Champaign Board of Education* [62] invalidated the so-called "released time" program of religious instruction in the schools of Champaign, Ill. Such plans of religious education had become widespread since their initial adoption around 1914. Under the Champaign plan, public school children, with the written consent of their parents, attended regular weekly classes in religious instruction. The classes were taught by Protestant, Catholic, and Jewish teachers, furnished by a religious council representing the various faiths. They were paid nothing from public funds but were subject to the approval and supervision of the school superintendent. Pupils not enrolled in the religious classes were required to continue their secular studies in other classrooms.

The Court held that this released time program fell "squarely under the ban" of the establishment of religion clause of the First Amendment, made applicable to the states by the Fourteenth, as construed in the Everson case. Two principal reasons were given for this holding: First, the program involved "a utilization of the tax-established and tax-supported public school system to aid religious groups to spread their faith." The Constitution forbids both state and federal governments from participation in the affairs of any religious organizations or groups, and vice versa. Second, the state was also aiding sectarian groups by helping to provide pupils for their religious classes through the state's compulsory public school machinery

[62] 333 U.S. 203 (1948).

The decision was greeted with a veritable storm of adverse criticism from interested church groups and from less partisan critics who believed that the Court had taken an extreme, if not an indefensible, position. Justice Black himself observed, in the Clauson case to be considered presently: "Probably few opinions from the Court in recent years have attracted more attention and stirred wider debate." [63]

It is not surprising that church groups attacked the Court's decision, for similar plans of religious instruction were in operation at this time in some 2000 school districts across the nation. But the decision was also denounced by scholars on historical and constitutional grounds. One of the most distinguished of these critics was Professor Edward S. Corwin, who declared that, "The historical record shows beyond peradventure that the core idea of 'an establishment of religion' comprises the idea of preference; and that an act of public authority favorable to religion cannot, without manifest falsification of history, be brought under the ban of that phrase." [64]

It is difficult to see how the Court could reach the conclusion it did in this case without reversing its ruling in the Everson case, for if there is any difference in the aid afforded the sectarian school in the two cases, it would clearly appear to be greater in the Everson case. In both cases the local government aided religious groups in securing attendance of pupils for religious instruction, but surely the use of schoolrooms for a short while once a week is less of a financial burden on the taxpayer—if, indeed, it is not too infinitesimal to be calculated—than the payment of bus fares. Moreover, the implication of Justice Black's argument, that in no circumstances and to no extent may public schoolrooms be used for religious instruction, would seem to be untenable. The long-accepted doctrine that no person should be taxed to support any religious sect was apparently aimed at the expenditure of public funds for the maintenance of church buildings, ministers' salaries, and other church work. "There was no thought in 1800 of prohibiting the use of microscopic portions of public funds for

[63] *Zorach* v. *Clauson,* 343 U.S. 317 (1952).

[64] "The Supreme Court as National School Board," *Law and Contemporary Problems,* Vol. 14 (Winter, 1949), p. 20.

heating, lighting and maintaining school rooms for short weekly periods of religious instruction of the nature provided in Champaign, Illinois." [65]

Justice Reed, in his lone dissent, relied primarily upon the accepted American tradition of state-church relations. He pointed out that there are many valid public aids to religion such as tax exemption of church property, the employment of chaplains in both houses of Congress and in the armed forces, and the training of veterans for the ministry at government expense in denominational schools, under the Servicemen's Readjustment Act of 1944. "Devotion to the great principles of religious liberty," he concluded, "should not lead us into a rigid interpretation of the Constitutional guarantee that conflicts with accepted habits of our people." To Justice Reed the established traditions of church-state relations determined the meaning of the establishment clause rather than what he regarded as dubious textual construction. He even expressed the view that "The phrase 'an establishment of religion,' may have been intended by Congress to be aimed only at a state church."

Taking Everson and McCollum together, it is apparent that the Court had worked itself into an untenable position. The welfare doctrine which was the basis of the ruling in Everson would logically justify almost any legislation and consequently deny any prohibitive effect to the establishment clause. On the other hand, the wall of separation doctrine was so applied in McCollum as to carry the implication that the First Amendment forbids all forms of public aid to religion, however general and nondiscriminatory.

Lowering the Wall of Separation

Whether or not it was consciously influenced by the criticism of the McCollum decision, the Court in 1952 reached the opposite conclusion with respect to substantially the same set of circumstances in *Zorach v. Clauson*.[66] In this case, a majority of six justices (Douglas, Vinson, and Burton, who had voted to invalidate the Champaign plan; Clark and Minton, who had come

[65] Lardner, *op. cit.*, p. 131.
[66] 343 U.S. 306 (1952).

on the Court after the McCollum decision; and Reed who had thought the Champaign plan valid) approved the New York state "dismissed-time" program of religious education. Under this plan the children were dismissed from school, on written request of their parents, to attend religious classes in religious centers off school grounds but during school hours. Pupils not dismissed were required to continue their studies in the school classrooms. Teachers were not allowed to announce the program to their students or to comment on attendance, but the churches made weekly reports to the schools, giving the names of pupils who had been released from school but had not reported for religious instruction.

The Court was here confronted with a dual issue: whether New York "by this system has either prohibited the free exercise of religion" or has made a law "respecting an establishment of religion." Justice Douglas, for the Court majority, quickly disposed of the first. It would, he declared, be obtuse reasoning to inject any issue of "free exercise" of religion into this case, since no one is compelled to take the religious instruction. In sustaining the New York program against the religious establishment claim, Justice Douglas first departed from the absolutist wall of separation doctrine applied in McCollum and grounded the Court's decision upon the well-established American tradition of state-church relations. In this connection, he pointed out the difficulty and absurdity of a rigid separation between church and state. The First Amendment does not require that church and state be hostile, suspicious, and unfriendly aliens to each other. If this were so,

Churches could not be required to pay even property taxes. Municipalities would not be permitted to render police or fire protection to religious groups. . . . Prayers in our legislative halls; the appeals to the Almighty in the messages of the Chief Executive; the proclamations making Thanksgiving Day a holiday; "So help me God" in our courtroom oaths—these and all other references to the Almighty that run through our laws, our public rituals, our ceremonies would be flouting the First Amendment.

It would be pushing the concept of separation to these extremes to hold the New York law unconstitutional. He continued: "We are a religious people whose institutions presuppose a Supreme Being," and "When the state encourages religious instruction or cooperates with religious authorities by adjusting the schedule of public events to sectarian needs, it follows the best of our traditions." Nothing in the Constitution requires government to show a callous indifference to religious groups. To do this would be to prefer those who believe in no religion over believers.

Justice Douglas did not stop here. He sought to reconcile this decision with the holding and theory of the McCollum case. The result of this was confusion and contradiction, as the dissenting justices were quick to point out. He thought that McCollum was distinguishable since there the public school classrooms were used for religious instruction, whereas here the public schools merely accommodate their schedules to a program of outside religious instruction. "We follow the McCollum case. But we cannot expand it to cover" the New York program, for "we cannot read into the Bill of Rights such a philosophy of hostility to religion."

Listing the prohibitions of the establishment clause of the First Amendment, Douglas stated:

Government may not finance religious groups nor undertake religious instruction nor blend secular and sectarian education nor use secular institutions to force one or some religion on any person. . . . It may not coerce anyone to attend church, to observe a religious holiday, or to take religious instruction.

It is, however, free to close its doors or suspend its operation for the benefit of those who wish to go to their religious sanctuary for worship or instruction. "No more than that is undertaken here." With respect to the last statement, it should be noted that the schools neither close their doors nor suspend their operations. Pupils who are not dismissed for religious instruction are compelled to continue their regular school activities. This is the crucial fact, which means that here, as in the Champaign plan, the educational system of the state is being adjusted to the promotion of sectarian objectives. Here, as there, the state is manipulating the "class room hours of its compulsory school machinery so as to channel children into sectarian classes."

Dissenting Justices Black, Frankfurter, and Jackson could not detect any substantial difference between this case and that of

McCollum. Justice Jackson characterized the attempt to differentiate between the two systems, on the ground that the New York plan provided for religious instruction off the school grounds, as "trivial almost to the point of cynicism, magnifying its nonessential details and disparaging compulsion which was the underlying reason for invalidity."

Justice Frankfurter, like his colleagues Jackson and Black, emphasized the compulsory aspects of the New York dismissed-time plan. "The pith of the case is that formalized religious instruction is substituted for other school activity which those who do not participate in the released-time program are compelled to attend."

SUMMARY ANALYSIS

It is clear that the Court, in the three important constitutional cases decided since 1947, has not succeeded in fixing the boundaries of the establishment clause of the First Amendment. Indeed, in certain areas it has rendered them more uncertain than ever. It is not unfair to say that confusion over the meaning of the establishment clause springs in considerable measure from confusion within the Court itself. The eleven opinions written in the three cases—3 majority, 2 concurring, and 6 dissenting—reveals a wide divergence of opinion regarding the spirit and scope of the clause.

The Everson and McCollum decisions, although based on the same wall of separation theory, had very different practical results. The confusion was confounded in the Clauson case when the opposite conclusion from McCollum was reached in a similar factual situation. The Clauson case, despite Justice Douglas' less than graceful effort to distinguish it from McCollum, actually scales down the high wall of separation erected by the Everson and McCollum opinions. It grounds the Court's conclusion in favor of released time religious instruction on the American tradition of state-church relations, elaborated by Justice Reed in his dissenting opinion in McCollum. Since this series of cases has not led to the formulation of a coherent and acceptable theory of interpretation, it is virtually certain that additional controversies will press upon the Court until the boundaries of religious establishment are more clearly drawn.

Established Principles

Despite uncertainties and confusion, the following points may be stated as more or less established:

1. Religious establishment, like free exercise of religion, has been absorbed into the due process clause of the Fourteenth Amendment as a restriction on the states. In this, the Court seems to regard freedom from establishment as an inseparable part of the free exercise of religion, and hence equally subject to the guardianship of the Supreme Court. It may be observed that the argument for inclusion of the concept of nonestablishment in the liberty of the Fourteenth Amendment is distinctly less convincing than that for the inclusion of religious exercise, if it is understood to forbid the states to render nondiscriminatory aid to religion where there is no restraint upon the free exercise of religion.

2. The American solution of the problem of church-state relations, so far as it has been worked out through judicial interpretation and experience, has been said to include these three principles:[67]

> *a.* free exercise of religion;
> *b.* separation of church and state;
> *c.* friendliness of government to the general cause of religion.

These principles find support in one or another of the foregoing cases, but so great are the diversities and apparent inconsistencies among the justices that they must be regarded as tentative. To what extent they will be modified by future judicial construction remains to be seen. Certain it is that many unsettled issues remain.

Unsettled Issues

Among the unsettled issues remaining from and growing out of the preceding cases are these:

1. Since the Clauson case, it is uncertain whether the Court has accepted the wall of separation theory of nonestablishment, or has wholly or partially abandoned it in favor of what may be called the "no preference" theory—a theory that the prohibition of laws "respecting an establishment of religion" merely forbids the granting of preferential aid to one religious sect or organization. Actually the Court seems to have substantially modified the wall of separation theory of Everson and McCollum in favor of a less rigid theory based on the American tradition of state-church relations. However, since the Court in Clauson did not repudiate the doctrine of McCollum, but rather

[67] See Anson Phelps Stokes, *Church and State in the United States* (New York, Harper, 1950), Vol. I, p. 37.

sought to reconcile the two cases, the issue remains an unsettled one.

2. It is not clear from the establishment cases whether and to what extent the states may render nonsectarian aid to sectarian schools with only incidental sectarian benefits. Does the logic of the Everson case, sustaining the constitutional validity of the expenditure of public funds for bus fares to parochial schools, and of the Cochran case, upholding the grant of secular textbooks to parochial schools, extend to all forms of nonsectarian aid to pupils of sectarian schools? The answer is important for public education.

3. It is likewise not clear whether and to what extent nondiscriminatory aid to religion in general is valid. Justice Black said in Everson that such aid was not valid; yet it is provided in various ways: the employment of chaplains in legislative bodies and in the armed forces, the exemption of church property from taxation, and the training of veterans for the ministry.

One final point may be stressed: Although the outermost boundaries of religious establishment have not been clearly marked, a fairly complete separation of church and state has been accepted and insisted on. The difficulty of the Court in maintaining the high wall of separation erected in the Everson and McCollum cases is doubtless due to a combination of the absence of judicial precedent in favor of such wall of separation and the opposing force of American thought and tradition with respect to the proper relation of spiritual and temporal affairs. The view is widely held not only in America but among the peoples of the entire western world that religion has had a profound effect upon democratic government, that by providing people with a philosophy of life, ethical standards, and spiritual ideals, it has greatly influenced the processes and aims of government. Lord Bryce expressed this view many years ago when he said, "History tells us . . . that free government has prospered best among religious people."[68]

Yet under the American theory of constitutional democracy, the benefits of religion can be most surely realized and the principle of liberty most effectively safeguarded by toleration of neither a state-dominated church nor a church-dominated state. Either of these alternatives would, in our concept, cause a serious restraint to be placed upon freedom of religious worship as well as upon other freedoms.

[68] *The American Commonwealth* (London, Macmillan, 1914), Vol. II, p. 794.

5   Political and Social Equality

The purpose of this chapter is to consider two general aspects of racial discrimination: discrimination as restrictive of political freedom, and discrimination as restrictive of the enjoyment of certain social advantages in relation to such questions as the acquisition and occupancy of property, transportation, and education.

POLITICAL FREEDOM: SUFFRAGE RESTRICTIONS

Political freedom implies, among other things, the right of general participation in the processes of political decision and control, and as bases for this right the enjoyment of the fundamental rights of free speech, press, assembly, and religion. The latter rights have been considered in the preceding chapters. Here, attention will first be focused on restrictions which have, from time to time, been imposed upon another and more concrete aspect of political freedom, namely, freedom of the suffrage. This, of course, involves consideration of the Fifteenth Amendment, as well as the Fourteenth.

During most of the time since the Fifteenth Amendment established the right of Negroes to vote, by declaring that "The right of citizens of the United States to vote shall not be denied or abridged by the United States or by any State on account of race, color, or previous condition of servitude," members of this race have nevertheless been effectively disfranchised by Southern states. The methods of circumvention employed by those states are too familiar to justify recounting in this brief study. Suffice it to say here that, up to 1915, restrictions on Negro suffrage had met with little resistance from the Supreme Court. For example, the literacy test, designed to bar the Negro from the ballot, was sustained by the Court in *Williams* v. *Mississippi*[1] in 1898.

Still, in 1915 the Court in *Guinn* v. *United States*[2] struck down the Oklahoma "grandfather clause" as a violation of the Fifteenth Amendment. This device, similar to those adopted earlier in some half dozen other Southern states, provided a loophole for the escape of illiterate whites from a literacy test for voting by exempting from the test those persons and their lineal descendants who were qualified to vote as of January 1, 1866, a date which would not apply to Negroes. Later efforts to circumvent the 1915 decision failed.[3] Nevertheless, these decisions did not dampen the zeal of states bent on disfranchising the Negro. The "white primary" and the poll tax proved to be effective weapons in this enterprise.)

The White Primary

The advent of the direct primary election toward the end of the last century and its widespread development in the first two decades of the present century furnished the South, ironically enough, with a new weapon against Negro suffrage. If the Negro could be barred from the Democratic primary, he would, of course, be effectively disfranchised, since in the South the choice made in the Democratic primary determines the outcome in the final election, which merely formalizes and legalizes the primary.

Inspiration for the first legislative prescription of the white primary apparently came from the inconclusive decision of the Supreme Court in *Newberry* v. *United States*,[4] in which Mr. Justice McReynolds, speaking for himself and three of his brethren, declared that a primary is no part of election and that the part of the Federal Corrupt Practices Act purporting to limit the expenditures of a Senatorial candidate in a primary was unconstitutional.[5]

Soon after this decision, the Texas legislature enacted a law barring Negroes from the polls in any Democratic primary in the

---

[1] 170 U.S. 213 (1898).
[2] 238 U.S. 347 (1915).
[3] *Lane* v. *Wilson,* 307 U.S. 268 (1939).
[4] 256 U.S. 232 (1921).
[5] Justice McKenna concurred in the judgment on other grounds.

state of Texas. The law was invalidated by the Supreme Court in
Nixon v. *Herndon* [6] as a violation of the equal protection of the
laws clause of the Fourteenth Amendment. The attempt to vest
the same power of discrimination in the state Central Committee
of the party failed because the Committee received its authority
to act from the legislature and hence was an agent of the state.[7]
But in *Grovey* v. *Townsend,*[8] in 1935, the Court upheld the exclusion of a Negro voter from the Democratic primary under the resolution of the state Democratic Convention without benefit of
statute. Here, the Court declared that to deny a vote in a primary
was a mere refusal of party membership in a private organization,
with which "the state need have no concern." The action was not
state action.

The great turning point came in 1941 when, in the Classic case,
the Court held that Section 4 of Article I of the Constitution au-
thorizes Congress to regulate primaries, as well as general elections, where the primary is by law an integral part of the procedure of choice (of a representative in Congress), or where in
fact the primary effectively controls the choice.[9] The Court also
held that it was the right of a qualified citizen of the United States
to vote in a Congressional primary and to have his vote counted
as cast.

It should be noted that this case did not settle the question as to
whether white people were free to exclude Negroes from primaries at which only state and local officers were chosen, or from
primaries for the selection of national officers which were not by
state law directly made a part of the state election machinery.
There was still *Grovey* v. *Townsend.*

In 1944 the Court in *Smith* v. *Allwright* [10] outlawed the white
primary as violative of the Fifteenth Amendment, and declared
that the constitutional right to be free from racial discrimination
in voting ". . . is not to be nullified by a state through casting its
electoral process in a form which permits a private organization
to practice racial discrimination in the election." The Court, after

[6] 273 U.S. 536 (1927).
[7] *Nixon* v. *Condon,* 286 U.S. 73 (1932).
[8] 295 U.S. 45 (1935).
[9] *United States* v. *Classic,* 313 U.S. 299, 318 (1941).
[10] 321 U.S. 649 (1944).

declaring that "It may be taken as a postulate that the right to vote in . . . a primary . . . without discrimination by the state . . . is a right secured by the Constitution," went on to hold that since by state law the primary was made an integral part of the state election machinery, the action of the party in excluding Negroes was action by the state and consequently in violation of the Fifteenth Amendment. Thus the controlling issue here, as in the Grovey case, was whether the Negro had been barred from the primary by *state* action. The Court held that he had, and consequently *Grovey* v. *Townsend* was overruled.

Although this decision greatly stimulated Negro participation in Southern primaries,[11] the resistance to it in most of the affected states was prompt and determined. These efforts at circumvention can be illustrated by the examples of South Carolina and Alabama, from both of which states issued important court decisions.[12]

South Carolina promptly repealed all statutory[13] and constitutional[14] laws relating to primaries, and the Democratic primary was thereafter conducted under rules prescribed by the Democratic Party. This bold attempt to circumvent the Allwright decision was struck down by the U. S. District Court in *Elmore* v. *Rice*,[15] on July 12, 1947; the decision was sustained by the Court of Appeals of the Fourth Circuit on December 30, 1947, and on April 19, 1948, the Supreme Court of the United States refused to review the latter ruling.[16]

Elmore was denied the right to vote in the Democratic primary under rules promulgated by the Democratic Convention limiting the right to vote in the primary to white persons. Both the District Court and the Court of Appeals ruled that the party and the primary were still serving as instruments of the state in the electoral process despite the repeal of all laws relating to primaries.[17]

[11] See O. D. Weeks, "The White Primary: 1944–1948," *American Political Science Review*, Vol. 42, No. 3 (June, 1948), pp. 500–510; also Donald S. Strong, "The Rise of Negro Voting in Texas," *ibid.*, pp. 510–512.

[12] For efforts in other Southern states, see Weeks, *op. cit.*

[13] Acts and Joint Resolutions, South Carolina, 1944, Sec. 2323.

[14] Constitution of South Carolina, Art. 2, Sec. 10.

[15] 72 F. Supp. 516 (1947).

[16] *Rice* v. *Elmore*, 165 F. 2d. 387 (1947); 68 S. Ct. 905 (1948).

[17] *Rice* v. *Elmore*, 165 F. 2d. 388.

It is worth noting that the primary involved in the Allwright case was conducted under the provisions of state law and not merely under party rules, as in this case. Here, the state had *permitted* the party to discriminate against the Negro voter in violation of the Constitution. The Appeals Court put the question before it sharply in this way:

> The question presented for our decision is whether by *permitting* [18] a party to take over a part of its election machinery, a state can avoid the provisions of the Constitution forbidding racial discrimination in elections and can deny to a part of the electorate because of race and color any effective voice in the government of the state. It seems perfectly clear that the question must be answered in the negative.[19] [Hence] no election machinery can be upheld if its purpose or effect is to deny to the Negro on account of his race or color any effective voice in the government of his country or the state or community wherein he lives.[20]

Undeterred, the Democratic Party authorities of South Carolina sought to evade the Elmore decision by vesting control of primaries in clubs to which Negroes were not admitted, and by requiring, for voting in the primaries, an oath which was particularly objectionable to Negroes. Among other things, they were to swear that they believed in the social and educational separation of the races. This effort failed in both the District Court [21] and the Court of Appeals [22] on the strength of the principle enunciated in the Elmore case.

The principle enunciated in the Elmore case was approved and applied by the Supreme Court of the United States in *Terry* v. *Adams*[23] in 1953. Fort Bend County, Texas, had for more than sixty years deprived Negroes of the ballot by setting up an association which included all white voters on the official list of the county and barred Negroes from membership. This organization, known as the Jaybird Democratic Association, claimed to be only a voluntary, private club with no connection whatever with the state political or elective machinery. Its ostensible duty was merely to pick candidates for recommendation to the regular party pri-

[18] Italics mine.   [19] *Rice* v. *Elmore,* 165 F. 2d. 389.
[20] *Ibid.,* p. 392.
[21] *Brown* v. *Baskin,* 78 F. Supp. 933 (1948).
[22] *Baskin* v. *Brown,* 174 F. 2d. 391 (1949).
[23] 345 U.S. 461 (1953).

mary. Expenses were met by assessing the candidates, and no reports or certification of candidates were made to any state or party officials. Here, Justice Black declared that the facts and findings of this case bring it squarely within the reasoning and holding of the Court of Appeals of the Fourth Circuit in the Elmore case, in which the principle was laid down "that no election machinery could be sustained if its purpose or effect was to deny Negroes on account of their race an effective voice in the governmental affairs of their country, state, or community."[24] Indeed, as already pointed out, essentially the same principle had previously been enunciated in *Smith* v. *Allwright,* when the Supreme Court said that the constitutional right to be free from racial discrimination in voting ". . . is not to be nullified by a state through casting its electoral process in a form which permits a private organization to practice racial discrimination in the election."[25]

The preceding cases, taken as a whole, would seem to indicate that no action of any group or organization which controls the choice of public officials and the decision of public issues, and the right of qualified citizens to participate in that choice and decision, is private action. Every attempt at preserving the substance of the white primary has ultimately failed in the courts, and it does not seem likely that future subterfuges will succeed except as delaying tactics.

Alabama refused to follow the example of South Carolina and to repeal her primary legislation as a method of circumventing *Smith* v. *Allwright,* apparently because of fear that primary elections could not be properly policed without state regulation. Instead, she sought to limit registration, and consequently voting, to "properly qualified persons." In 1946 the so-called Boswell Amendment to the Constitution of Alabama was adopted, providing that only persons who can "understand and explain" any article of the Constitution of the United States, who are possessed of "good character," and who understand "the duties and obligations of good citizenship under a republican form of government" may qualify as electors.[26]

---

[24] *Rice* v. *Elmore,* 165 F. 2d. 389, 392.
[25] 321 U.S. 644 at 664.
[26] Section 181 of the Constitution of Alabama, as amended (1946).

Under the statutory law the applicant for registration must "understand and explain" the duties and obligations of good citizenship to the reasonable satisfaction of the boards of registrars for the several counties of the state.[27]

It is, of course, not surprising, that a Federal district court found that the amendment was intended as a grant of arbitrary power to evade the decision of the Supreme Court in *Smith* v. *Allwright* and to restrict voting on the basis of color, that evidence showed it had in fact been arbitrarily administered for the purpose of excluding Negro applicants from the franchise, whereas white applicants with comparable qualifications were accepted, and that as a rule only Negroes were required to submit to the tests. Thus the amendment, "both in its object and the manner of its administration is unconstitutional because it violates the Fifteenth Amendment."[28] The Supreme Court refused to overrule this decision.[29]

Constitutional Aspects of the Poll Tax

There are now only five Southern states—Alabama, Arkansas, Mississippi, Virginia, and Texas—which make the payment of a poll tax prerequisite to the exercise of the suffrage.[30] The requirements originally were designed primarily to disfranchise the Negro, but in later years they often operated to disfranchise whites as well. On the national level, efforts to eliminate the poll tax as a suffrage requirement have been confined largely to two methods: (1) invalidation by the courts, and (2) failing in this, the outlawry of the tax by act of Congress. Each method will be examined briefly.

The contention that a poll tax as a qualification for voting in a state or federal election is unlawful was brought before the Supreme Court in *Breedlove* v. *Suttles* in 1937. The plaintiff had been excluded from both state and national elections because of failure to pay a poll tax imposed by the state of Georgia. Against the contention of Breedlove that the privilege of voting for federal officials

[27] Title 17, Sec. 21, Code of Alabama, 1940.
[28] *Davis* v. *Schnell,* 81 F. Supp. 872 (1949).
[29] 69 S. Ct. 747 (1949).
[30] Technically, it could be argued that Tennessee should be added to the list, but the legislature of that state has made such extensive exemptions as to amount to repeal of the tax. See V. O. Key, Jr., *Politics, Parties and Pressure Groups* (New York, Crowell, 1952), 3rd ed., pp. 622–623.

is one to which he is entitled under the Fourteenth Amendment, the Court concluded that to make the payment of poll taxes a prerequisite of voting is not to deny any privilege or immunity protected by the Fourteenth Amendment. "The privilege of voting," said Mr. Justice Butler for the Court, "is not derived from the United States, but is conferred by the state and, save as restrained by the Fifteenth and Nineteenth Amendments and other provisions of the Federal Constitution, the state may condition suffrage as it deems appropriate. . . ."[31] Incidentally Mr. Justice Butler's language is in error as applied to the privilege of voting for members of the Congress. To be sure, the qualifications of electors of members of the Congress are defined by state law, as will be noted presently, but the right to vote for such officials is derived from the Constitution of the United States.[32]

Later cases involving the poll tax as a requirement for the exercise of the suffrage regard the matter as conclusively determined in *Breedlove* v. *Suttles*.[33]

Federal Anti-Poll Tax Legislation

Since 1939 more than a half-dozen bills designed to prohibit the imposition of a poll tax as a prerequisite to voting in a primary or other election for national officers have passed the House of Representatives but have failed in the Senate through death in committee or Senatorial filibuster, chiefly the latter. All are virtually identical in substance. A typical example is the one introduced by Senator Humphrey in the First Session of the Eighty-second Congress on June 25, 1951. Section 3 of this bill makes it unlawful "to levy, collect or require the payment of any poll tax" as a condition of voting in any national election, and declares that any such action "shall be deemed an interference with the manner of holding such elections, an abridgment of the right and privilege of citizens of the United States to vote" for national officers "and an obstruction of the operation of the Federal Government."[34]

[31] *Breedlove* v. *Suttles*, 302 U.S. 277 (1937).
[32] Ex parte *Yarbrough*, 110 U.S. 651 (1884); *United States* v. *Classic*, 313 U.S. 299, 315 (1941).
[33] *Pirtle* v. *Brown*, 118 F. 2d. 218; *Butler* v. *Thompson*, 97 F. Supp. 17 (1951). In both these cases certiorari was denied by the Supreme Court.
[34] S. 1734, 82d Cong., 1st Sess.

The assumption of this bill that the poll tax requirement is not a qualification for the exercise of the suffrage but rather an interference with the manner of holding elections seems to be untenable. Since most of the state constitutions of 1787 required poll tax payments or property tax payments as a condition of voting,[35] it would seem reasonable that the framers of the federal Constitution had these provisions in mind when they stipulated that the electors for members of the House of Representatives should possess the qualifications "requisite for electors for the most numerous branch of the state Legislature." Thus the constitutionality of proposed anti-poll tax legislation would seem to be dubious at best.[36]

Political Rights of Federal Employees

As early as 1882,[37] the Supreme Court sustained an act of Congress, which forbade certain classes of officers of the United States to request from, give to, or receive from any other officer money, property, or anything of value for political purposes.[38]

In 1939, Congress enacted the so-called Hatch Act, Sec. 9 (*a*) of which provides that no employee in the executive branch of the federal government "shall take any active part in political management or in political campaigns," and subjects any one violating this section to immediate removal from his office or position.[39] A divided Court held this law constitutional in a case[40] involving one Poole, a roller in the Mint, who was at the same time serving as a ward executive committeeman of his political party and as a worker at the polls. To the contention that the statute violated the employee's First Amendment rights of free speech and press, necessary elements of political activity, the Court replied that such restrictions clearly fall within the range of Congressional power to safeguard the efficiency and integrity of the federal service.

[35] F. N. Thorpe, *Charters and Constitutions* (59th Cong., 2d Sess., House Doc. 357), pp. 2595, 2630, 2790, 3096. Also 6 Thorpe, *ibid.*, 3248.

[36] But see R. A. Hogenson, "Anti-Poll Tax Legislation and the Federal Constitution," *George Washington Law Review*, Vol. 11 (December, 1949), p. 77.

[37] Ex parte *Curtis*, 106 U.S. 371 (1882).

[38] St. 143, Sec. 6 (1876).

[39] 53 Stat. 1147 (1939).

[40] *United Public Workers* v. *Mitchell*, 330 U.S. 75 (1947).

A later amendment, which constitutes Sec. 12(*a*) of this act, provides that:

> no officer or employee of any state or local agency whose principal employment is in connection with any activity which is financed in whole or in part by loans or grants made by the United States or by any Federal Agency shall . . . take any active part in political management or in political campaigns.

Acting under the authority of this section, the Civil Service Commission of the United States ordered the removal from office of a member of the Oklahoma State Highway Commission, who was at the same time serving as chairman of the state Central Committee of the Democratic Party and was in charge of arrangements for a "victory dinner" for the purpose of raising money for the party. In upholding the removal, the Court rejected the contention of the state of Oklahoma that the coercive effect of the authorization to withhold money allocated to a state violated its reserved power under the Tenth Amendment, and declared that Congress had the right to fix the conditions under which the states shall receive federal loans or grants-in-aid. Oklahoma was free to choose between dismissing the commissioner and refusing to accept the federal funds.[41]

These cases are based on the assumption, which apparently enjoys wide support, that Congress may, as a condition of employment, impose upon those citizens who are public employees restrictions that it may not impose on other citizens. The general right to engage in political activity does not carry with it a special right to public employment.

RACIAL DISCRIMINATION AND EQUAL PROTECTION OF THE LAWS

Many Supreme Court cases since 1937 have involved the issue of racial discrimination. Only a few of these, deemed most significant as charting doctrinal trends, can be considered here. It may be noted, however, that these cases, taken as a whole, reflect a consistent, though sometimes cautious, tendency on the part of the Court during this period so to interpret the Fourteenth Amend-

---

[41] *Oklahoma* v. *United States Civil Service Commission,* 330 U.S. 127 (1947).

ment and other pertinent provisions of the Constitution as to insure genuine equality of public treatment to racial minorities.

Doctrinal progress in this direction can be illustrated by a brief review of cases concerning segregation with respect to: (1) the acquisition and occupancy of real property; (2) access to public transportation facilities; and (3) the right to equal educational opportunity.

Segregation in Residential Areas

Three cases,[42] all decided since the beginning of 1948, have gone far to free the colored race from earlier restrictions with respect to the acquisition, occupancy, and conveyance of real property. This emancipation has come about largely through an expansion of the concept of state action on the part of the Supreme Court. It had been held in the Civil Rights cases,[43] as early as 1883, that the Fourteenth Amendment does not forbid private discrimination against the Negro. This doctrine was, of course, applicable in decisions holding that private property owners may covenant with one another not to sell or lease their property to Negroes. These "restrictive covenants," as they were called, became more important after the Supreme Court ruled in *Buchanan* v. *Warley*[44] in 1917 that an ordinance of Louisville, Ky., setting up exclusive residential areas based on color, was in violation of the Fourteenth Amendment. Such segregation of races in residential areas could still be effected through private covenants if violation of the covenants could be enforced in the courts. In 1926 private covenants forbidding the transfer of land to, or its use by, Negroes for a period of years was unanimously sustained in *Corrigan* v. *Buckley*[45] on the ground that the discrimination was not effected by state action.

The Supreme Court avoided meeting this issue in subsequent cases for more than two decades.[46] In 1948, however, the Court

[42] *Shelley* v. *Kraemer*, 334 U.S. 1 (1948); *Hurd* v. *Hodge*, 334 U.S. 24 (1948); *Barrows* v. *Jackson*, 346 U.S. 249 (1953).

[43] 109 U.S. 3 (1883).

[44] 245 U.S. 60 (1917).

[45] 271 U.S. 323 (1926).

[46] *Hansberry* v. *Lee*, 311 U.S. 32 (1940); *Mays* v. *Burgess* 147 F. 2d. 869 (App. D.C. 1944; cert. denied, 325 U.S. 868 (1945).

held that racially restrictive covenants may not be enforced in equity by state courts against Negro purchasers.[47] Although such covenants are valid as between private persons, enforcement by the state courts constitutes a denial of the equal protection of the laws. The fact that the state uses its courts to give effect to the discriminatory private contract makes the state a party to the action. In *Hurd* v. *Hodge*,[48] decided the same day, restrictive covenants in the District of Columbia were held equally unenforceable in federal equity courts. Here the Court sidestepped the constitutional issue and held that restrictive covenants are prohibited by the section of the Civil Rights Act of 1866, which provides that "all citizens of the United States shall have the same right, in every state and territory, as is enjoyed by white citizens thereof to inherit, purchase, lease, sell, hold and convey real and personal property. . . ."

In the later case of *Barrows* v. *Jackson*,[49] the Court went further and ruled by a 6 to 1 vote that a state court may not, for the same reason as set forth in the Shelley case, take jurisdiction of a damage suit at law for breach of the restrictive covenant brought by one white covenanter against another. For state courts to entertain such damage suits amounts to state encouragement of the use of restrictive covenants, said Mr. Justice Minton, and thus coerces the property owner to continue to use his property in a discriminatory manner. It is, therefore, the state's choice that he either observe the covenant or suffer damages. These cases would seem to invalidate any state assistance to private efforts to enforce racial discrimination with respect to the use or conveyance of property. Nevertheless, the Supreme Court in 1950 refused to review a decision of the New York Court of Appeals, holding that a private housing corporation could exclude Negroes from a housing project constructed with the assistance of the state's power of eminent domain and city tax exemption for twenty-five years.[50]

It appears from a more recent case[51] that where the state court

[47] *Shelley* v. *Kraemer*, 334 U.S. 1 (1948).
[48] 334 U.S. 24 (1948).
[49] 346 U.S. 249 (1953).
[50] *Daisy* v. *Stuyvesant*, 299 N.Y. 512 (1949); 339 U.S. 981 (1950).
[51] *Black* v. *Cutlers Laboratories*, 351 U.S. 292 (1956); see also *Rice* v. *Sioux City Park*, 349 U.S. 70 (1955).

merely refused to interfere with discrimination arising from a private agreement, the action of the court is not state action as in Shelley and Barrows where the agreement had been ineffective without judicial intervention. In these cases the action of the court had the effect of forcing discrimination on parties willing to deal on a nondiscriminatory basis.

Segregation in Transportation Facilities

Cases involving segregation in public transportation facilities have been decided under such diverse constitutional provisions as the commerce and equal protection clauses. Under both provisions the Supreme Court has followed a tortuous and confusing course in the determination of the difficult questions which have come before it. In the first Jim Crow case,[52] the Court in 1878 held invalid, as a burden on interstate commerce, a Louisiana reconstruction statute forbidding steamboats on the Mississippi River from segregating passengers according to race. A Negro woman was refused accommodations in the white cabins on a Mississippi steamer traveling from New Orleans to Vicksburg, Miss. This, the Court said, was a subject requiring uniformity of regulation which only Congress could adopt, and in the absence of Congressional regulation the carrier was free to enforce such regulations for the arrangements of his passengers as he might deem "most for the interest of all concerned."

Some years later, however, the Court sustained laws requiring segregation within a state on the ground that they regulated only intrastate commerce and hence imposed no burden on interstate commerce.[53]

In *Plessy* v. *Ferguson*[54] in 1896, the equal protection clause of the Fourteenth Amendment likewise failed as a bulwark against Jim Crow legislation. Here a Louisiana statute providing separate but equal accommodations for white and colored persons on railroads in the state was held not to deny equal protection of the laws. On the contrary, it was a valid exercise of the state police power to preserve public peace and good order.

[52] *Hall* v. *De Cuir*, 95 U.S. 485 (1878).
[53] *Louisville, No. O. & T. R. Co.* v. *Mississippi*, 133 U.S. 587 (1890).
[54] 163 U.S. 537 (1896).

Justice Brown rested the conclusions of the Court largely on the observation that the underlying fallacy in the argument of the Negro plaintiff consisted in

the assumption that the enforced separation of the two races stamps the colored race with a badge of inferiority. If this be so, it is not by reason of anything found in the act, but solely because the colored race chooses to put that construction upon it. [Justice Harlan declared in dissent that] there can be no doubt but that segregation has been enforced as a means of subordinating the Negro. . . . [and] That the thin disguise of "equal" accommodation . . . will not mislead anyone nor atone for the wrong this day done. . . .

Thus segregation with respect to transportation facilities became constitutionally reconcilable with equality, and the formula of "separate but equal" operated for more than a half-century to perpetuate what later came to be regarded as a gap between the theory and practice of equality of the races before the law. To be sure, the separate accommodations must be equal, but the Court until the 1930's was extremely lenient in its construction of the requirements of equality. This was especially true with respect to equality of educational opportunity, as will be seen shortly.

After the Plessy decision, the opponents of segregation again turned to the commerce clause, since the De Cuir case had not actually been overruled. But it was not until half a century after Plessy that the commerce clause was successfully invoked against segregation in public transportation. However, there had been a tendency in some earlier cases to interpret the requirements of equality more rigidly. For example, in *McCabe* v. *Atchison*[55] in 1914, an Oklahoma statute which permitted carriers to provide sleeping and dining cars for white persons only was held invalid, despite the legislative recognition that there would be little demand for them by colored people.

Finally, in *Mitchell* v. *United States*,[56] decided in 1941, the Court construed the interstate commerce act to require equal accommodation for Negroes. A. W. Mitchell, a Negro Congressman from Chicago, traveled from Chicago to Hot Springs, Ark., on a ticket which entitled him to Pullman accommodations. When the

[55] 235 U.S. 151 (1914).
[56] 313 U.S. 80 (1941).

train crossed the Arkansas border, he was ejected from the Pullman car and forced to ride in a day coach reserved for colored passengers. The railroad purported to provide Negroes with separate but equal facilities required by the Arkansas statute, by permitting Negroes who wished Pullman accommodations to buy drawing room space at ordinary Pullman rates. No such space was available on this occasion. It was not disputed that there was little demand for Pullman space by Negroes. Mitchell filed a complaint with the Interstate Commerce Commission, claiming discriminatory treatment in violation of the Interstate Commerce Act. The Commission dismissed his complaint, but the Supreme Court, speaking through Chief Justice Hughes, unanimously held that Mitchell was entitled to relief under the federal statute which forbids discriminatory treatment by railroads on account of race. The test of equality was not met, the Court pointed out, since Negroes with first class tickets were given accommodations equal to those afforded white persons traveling on second class tickets. Allowing Negroes to buy drawing room space, if available, similarly did not meet the test, nor is inequality to be justified by the small number of Negroes desiring Pullman accommodations. It is the individual who is entitled to the equal protection of the law.

It is clear, of course, that neither of the two preceding cases challenged the constitutionality of segregation in interstate commerce. They do, however, reveal a new determination on the part of the Court that the constitutional requirement of equality shall be meaningful. Then, in 1946, the Court in *Morgan* v. *Virginia*[57] reverted to the De Cuir doctrine and held invalid a Virginia statute requiring segregation on all buses in interstate as well as intrastate commerce. The case involved the prosecution of a Negro woman who refused to move to the back of the bus on the request of the driver, when traveling from Virginia to Baltimore. Reversing the state Supreme Court of Appeals which had affirmed the passenger's conviction, the Supreme Court of the United States held the segregation law to be a burden on interstate commerce in matters where uniformity is necessary. As indicated, the Court here followed *Hall* v. *De Cuir,* and in doing so opened the way,

[57] 328 U.S. 373 (1946).

as Mr. Justice Burton suggested in dissent, for other suits in eighteen states where segregation was prohibited. So, in *Bob-Lo Excursion Co.* v. *Michigan*,[58] the Court found the commerce clause being invoked to protect discrimination. In this case the Michigan Civil Rights Act was invoked against an amusement park company, which operated a boat between Detroit and an island on the Canadian side of the Detroit River and which refused to transport a Negro girl to the island in company with white girls. The defense was that the state law could not be validly applied to foreign commerce. The majority of the Court held that, although the commerce was technically foreign, the Canadian island was so close to Detroit as to be an amusement adjunct of the Michigan city. De Cuir and Morgan did not involve such "locally insulated" situations. The judicial drive against segregation in transportation was continued in the 1950 case of *Henderson* v. *United States*,[59] but again the Court sidestepped the constitutional issue of whether segregation as such denied equality. The Court found that the practice of the Southern Railway Co. in assigning one table in the dining car exclusively to Negroes, separated by a curtain from ten other tables reserved for whites, violated the provisions of the amended Interstate Commerce Act, which made it "unlawful for any railway engaged in interstate commerce to subject any particular person . . . to any undue or unreasonable prejudice or disadvantage in any respect whatever."[60] The Court rejected the argument that the segregation was rendered reasonable by the possibility that white passengers could be subjected to the same disadvantage as Negroes.

Despite the Court's insistence upon a more genuine equality in these later transportation cases, it carefully avoided making any assault upon the citadel of "separate but equal." This historic feat was reserved for the field of education.

It may be stated at this point that, after the segregation case of *Brown* v. *Board of Education*,[61] which will be discussed presently, the Court held, in a series of *per curiam* opinions,[62] segregation

[58] 333 U.S. 28 (1948).   [59] 339 U.S. 816 (1950).
[60] 54 Stat. 902, 49 U.S.C. §3(1), 1946.
[61] 349 U.S. 294 (1954).
[62] *Owen et al.* v. *Browder et al.*, 352 U.S. 903; *Mayor and City Council of Baltimore* v. *Dawson*, 350 U.S. 877; *Holmes* v. *City of Atlanta*, 350 U.S. 879.

on intrastate buses, on public golf courses, public beaches, parks, and playgrounds to be a denial of the equal protection of the laws clause of the Fourteenth Amendment. In all these cases the Court simply cited *Brown* v. *Board of Education.*

Segregation in Education

With *Missouri* ex rel *Gaines* v. *Canada* [63] in 1938, the Supreme Court started on a course of doctrinal liberalism in the interpretation of the equal protection clause in relation to educational opportunity, which carried it without deviation to the climactic school segregation decisions of May 17, 1954. From this case on, the Court consistently enforced a much more rigid test of equality. It insisted on reviewing more critically the facts of the cases brought before it to ascertain whether equality was in truth afforded. In the education cases decided during the nearly sixty years between *Plessy* v. *Ferguson* and the school segregation cases of 1954, the Supreme Court at first evaded the separate but equal issue,[64] then apparently tacitly accepted it without confronting it head-on, and finally interpreted the "equal" side of the formula so rigidly as to make it virtually impossible to comply with it under segregation.

Under the Plessy doctrine, which was never directly ruled on by the Supreme Court in an education case until the cases of 1954, public segregation is valid only if the separate facilities provided for the races are equal. Up to 1938, the Court had been as lenient in construing the requirements of "equality" in the school systems of the segregated states as it had been with respect to public transportation facilities. Indeed, the disingenuousness of the protection afforded by the separate but equal formula is even more apparent in the field of education than in other areas. It is common knowledge that Negro schools in segregated states have been conspicuously inferior to white schools, and only in recent years have they approached, and in some cases achieved, substantial equality. For many years, as indicated above, the Supreme Court was able to avoid recognition of this fact. In the first school case to reach the Court after *Plessy* v. *Ferguson,* the

[63] 305 U.S. 337 (1938).
[64] See *Cumming* v. *County Board of Education,* 175 U.S. 528 (1899).

Court found no denial of the protection of equal laws in the action of a local school board, which discontinued a Negro high school for economic reasons while continuing to operate the existing high school for whites.[65] The fact of segregation was not challenged. Negro taxpayers simply sought to restrain the school board from using tax money to support white high schools until equal facilities for Negroes were provided.

In 1908, the Court sustained a Kentucky statute, even as applied to a private college, forbidding the teaching of white and colored persons in the same institution. The Court was again able to escape passing on the segregation problem by basing its decision on the right of the state to withhold privileges from one of its own created corporations.

In *Gong Lum* v. *Rice*, in 1927, the Court held that an American-born Chinese girl could be compelled, without denial of the protection of equal laws, to attend a school for colored children in a neighboring school district, contrary to her desire to attend the nearby school for white children. Again the separate but equal doctrine was not challenged. The petitioner took the position that, because there were no separate schools for Mongolians, she was entitled to enter the white public schools in her own district in preference to the Negro schools in another district. Her counsel advanced this interesting argument: "The white race creates for itself a privilege that it denies to other races; exposes the children of other races to risks and dangers to which it would not expose its own children. This is discrimination." But Chief Justice Taft treated the interesting equal protection issue posed here as though it had already been well settled by the Court. If the question were new it would call for "full argument and consideration," he said, but he thought "it is the same question which has been many times decided to be within the constitutional power of the state legislature to settle without intervention of the federal courts. . . ." It should be noted that the precedents cited by the Chief Justice are either state or lower federal court decisions. The Supreme Court had never ruled directly on the issue of segregation and equal protection in public educational institutions, al-

[65] *Cumming* v. *County Board of Education,* 175 U.S. 528 (1899).

though it had apparently received the blessing of the Court in *dicta.*

With the Gaines case in 1938, the Court began to take much more seriously the "equal" part of the separate but equal formula.[66] Here, the Court held that Missouri had denied the protection of equal laws to Gaines, a Negro, in refusing him admission to the University of Missouri Law School when the state had provided no substantially equal facilities for Negroes within its jurisdiction. Missouri, like other Southern states, had provided for payment of tuition fees of qualified Negro citizens of the state to the law schools of unsegregated states, and insisted that by this arrangement it had met the separate but equal requirement.

The contention was flatly rejected by the Court. Chief Justice Hughes, speaking for the Court, asserted that equal protection requires Missouri to provide equal facilities for Negroes and whites within its own boundaries. The provision for the payment of tuition fees in another state does not remove the discrimination, for "the obligation of the state to give the protection of equal laws can be performed only where its laws operate, that is, within its own jurisdiction."

The state's argument that there was little demand for legal education on the part of Negroes in Missouri had no bearing on the issue. The right asserted by the petitioner, said the Court, was a personal one and could not be abridged because no other Negroes sought the same opportunity.

The big surge toward repudiation of the separate but equal theory came in 1950, when the Court in two vitally significant cases unanimously and emphatically condemned racial segregation in the professional and graduate schools of state universities. In the first of these cases, *Sweatt* v. *Painter,*[67] the Court held that the barring of a Negro applicant from the University of Texas Law School had deprived him of the equal protection of the laws, even though Texas had, at considerable expense, provided a separate law school for Negroes within the state. In effect, the Court found that a segregated law school for Negroes could not provide them with equal educational opportunities. In reaching such a con-

[66] 305 U.S. 337 (1938).
[67] 339 U.S. 629 (1950).

clusion, against the argument of the state of Texas that the new law school for Negroes afforded equal facilities, the Court relied heavily on "those qualities which are incapable of objective measurement but which make for greatness in a law school." Chief Justice Vinson contrasted the two law schools by such standards as the reputation of the faculties, the size of the student bodies and libraries, the influence and prestige of the large body of alumni of the University Law School as against the single alumnus of the Negro law school, the experience of the administration, and the traditions and prestige of the University Law School in general. The Court also pointed to the practical disadvantages incident to the state's exclusion from the Negro law school of 85 per cent of the population of the state, including most of the lawyers, judges, jurors, witnesses, and other officials with whom Negro lawyers would necessarily have to deal in the practice of their profession.

In short, legal education equivalent to that offered by the state to white students was not available to Negroes in a separate law school as offered by the state. Nevertheless, the Court, adhering to the principle of deciding constitutional questions only in the context of the particular case before it, explicitly refused to affirm or re-examine the doctrine of *Plessy* v. *Ferguson*. It simply held that the equal protection clause of the Fourteenth Amendment required Sweatt to be admitted to the University of Texas Law School. Yet, it raised the standard of equality to such a level as to make it virtually impossible for any scheme of segregation to meet the test of constitutionality.

The Sweatt ruling was reinforced in the McLaurin case,[68] where the Court held that enforced segregation of the scholastic activities of a Negro graduate student, who had been admitted to the state university under Court order, was a denial of equal protection in that it handicapped him in the effective pursuit of his graduate studies. McLaurin was segregated from his fellow students with respect to seating arrangements in the university dining room, the library, and the classroom. These restrictions, said Chief Justice Vinson, "impair and inhibit his ability to study, to engage in discussion and exchange views with other students, and, in

[68] *McLaurin* v. *Oklahoma State Regents,* 339 U.S. 637 (1950).

general, to learn his profession." To the argument that McLaurin's fellow students might refuse to associate with him regardless of state discrimination, the Court retorted that this was irrelevant.

There is a vast difference—a constitutional difference—between restrictions imposed by the state which prohibit the intellectual commingling of students, and the refusal of students to commingle where the state presents no such bar.

Here the Court leaned even more heavily upon psychological and other intangible factors than in the Sweatt case, but again it refused to re-examine the Plessy case. In both these cases, the Court had, in effect, rejected segregation without repudiating or overruling the separate but equal doctrine. It was able to do this because there was before it in these, as in earlier cases, a specific racial discrimination within the pattern of segregation, and it could therefore grant relief to the Negro plaintiffs without the necessity of re-examining the separate but equal doctrine. Nevertheless, these two cases had the effect of divesting *Plessy* v. *Ferguson* of its constitutional substance and paved the way for the historic segregation decisions of May 17, 1954.

The School Segregation Cases

The Supreme Court's consideration of these cases was marked by extraordinary caution and deliberation. When the Court convened in the fall of 1952, five cases in which racial segregation of children in public schools was squarely challenged as unconstitutional awaited its consideration. Four arose from the states of South Carolina, Virginia, Delaware, and Kansas, and one from the District of Columbia. After hearing argument on the five cases in December, 1952, the Court failed to reach a decision in the 1952 term, and on June 8, 1953, ordered the cases restored to the docket for re-argument in the 1953 term. On this occasion the Court resorted to the unusual practice of requesting counsel to provide answers, if possible, to certain important questions posed by the Court.

Essentially what the Court wanted to know was: first, whether there was historical evidence to show the intentions of those who had proposed and approved the Fourteenth Amendment, with respect to its effect upon racial segregation in the public schools; second, if the Court should find segregation in violation of the Fourteenth Amendment, what sort of decree could and should be issued to effect an orderly termination of segregation? Especially on this point, may the Court, "in the exercise of its equity powers, permit an effective gradual adjustment . . . from existing segregated systems to a system not based on color distinctions?"

The cases were re-argued in December, 1953, with elaborate briefs on the intention of the framers and ratifiers of the Fourteenth Amendment. The Court still proceeded with caution and deliberation and did not hand down its decision until May 17, 1954.

The four cases arising from the aforementioned states were considered in a consolidated opinion in the style of *Brown* v. *Board of Education of Topeka*.[69] In these cases the question of the constitutional consistency of racial segregation and equal protection of the laws was directly presented to the Court. Findings of fact in the lower courts showed that colored and white schools had been equalized, or were being equalized, so far as tangible factors were concerned. The charge made here was that public segregation *per se* denied equal protection.[70]

Chief Justice Warren, again emphasizing the intangible factors of Sweatt and McLaurin, declared for the unanimous Court that such considerations apply with added force to children in grade and high schools. To separate children of the minority group from others of similar age and qualifications solely because of their race creates a feeling of inferiority as to their status in the community, and this sense of inferiority affects the motivation of the child to learn. Hence the Supreme Court agreed with the Kansas court that "Segregation with the sanction of law . . . has a tendency to retard the education and mental development of Negro children and to deprive them of some of the benefits they would receive in a racially integrated school system." The Court, there-

[69] 347 U.S. 483 (1954).

[70] Segregation in the District of Columbia was held in *Bolling* v. *Sharpe* (347 U.S. 497) to violate the due process of law clause of the Fifth Amendment.

fore, concludes that the doctrine of separate but equal [71] has no place in the field of public education, that "separate educational facilities are inherently unequal," and that the plaintiffs here involved "have been deprived of the equal protection of the laws guaranteed by the Fourteenth Amendment."

In reaching this conclusion, the Court considered "public education in the light of its full development and its present place in American life throughout the Nation." "In approaching this problem," said the Chief Justice, "we cannot turn the clock back to 1868 when the Amendment was adopted, or even to 1896 when *Plessy* v. *Ferguson* was written." Moreover, the historical evidence submitted by counsel and supplemented by the Court's own investigation was inconclusive as to the intended effect of the Fourteenth Amendment on public education.

Whatever the difficulties of adjustment to this historic decision (and the events since 1955 indicate that they are many, serious, and even explosive), an opposite decision would have placed the Court in an awkward position both morally and constitutionally. Developments with respect to segregation in both transportation and education had pointed to the decision reached by the Court. Otherwise some backtracking on Sweatt and McLaurin would have been necessary, and the Court would have found itself in the absurd position of using the commerce clause to prevent racial segregation in transportation and rejecting equal protection and due process for the same purpose in public education.

The Court did not issue a decree putting its decision into effect on May 17, 1954; rather, it ordered the cases restored to the docket for further argument on the nature of the decrees by which its decision might be given effect.

In its implementing decision of May 31, 1955,[72] the Court pointed out that its earlier opinions "declaring the fundamental principle that racial discrimination in public education is unconstitutional are incorporated herein by reference" and declared that "all provisions of Federal, state, or local law requiring or permit-

[71] For a lucid discussion of the origin, application, and repudiation of this doctrine, see Robert J. Harris, "The Constitution, Education, and Segregation," *Temple Law Quarterly*, Vol. 29, No. 4 (Summer, 1956), pp. 409–433.
[72] *Brown* v. *Board of Education*, 349 U.S. 294 (1955).

ting such discrimination must yield to this principle." The District Courts, to which the cases were remanded, were directed to require that the school authorities "make a prompt and reasonable start towards full compliance" with the Court's May 17, 1954, ruling. Once such a start were made in good faith, the Courts might afford additional time to carry out the ruling. In effecting a gradual transition from segregated to nonsegregated schools, the District Courts

may consider problems related to the physical condition of the school plant, the school transportation system, personnel, revision of school districts and attendance areas into compact units to achieve a system determining admission to the public schools on a non-racial basis, and revision of local laws and regulations which may be necessary in solving the foregoing problems.

Although it is clear from the language of the Court that all these procedures must point in the direction of compliance with the Court's ruling at the earliest practicable date, there is no indication that reasonable time would not be afforded for adjustment to difficult local situations. The Court's opinion recognized diversity of local conditions, and did not contemplate uniform compliance as of a given date. However, the Court did demand a prompt and reasonable start toward good-faith compliance.

Many moderate but largely silent people regard it as unfortunate that the breathing spell afforded by the Court for assessing problems and planning methods of adjustment to its far-reaching decision has been so defiantly exploited by the constituted leadership of some affected states. Too often, they feel, the appeal has been, not to the law-abiding instincts of the people, but to their prejudices, their hates, and their fears.

Reactions in the affected states range all the way from prompt steps toward compliance in some border states, to hostile gestures toward the Supreme Court, as for example in Virginia, to outright declarations of nullification in some states of the deep South. Among the formal declarations of hostility may be mentioned the "Interposition" resolution of the Virginia legislature and the "Declaration of Constitutional Principles," issued on March 11, 1956, by some 100 Southern Congressmen from 11 Southern states.

The first document is an official resolution passed by an overwhelming majority of both houses of the General Assembly of Virginia. In this resolution, the state is said to "interpose its sovereignty" against the decision of the Court, thereby raising "a question of contested power."[73] The legislators pledge their "firm intention" to take all measures "honorably, legally, and constitutionally available to us, to resist this illegal encroachment upon our sovereign powers, and to urge our sister states" to assist in the matter.

The second of these documents, commonly known as the Southern Manifesto,[74] is not, of course, an official document but a statement of a minority of the members of the Senate and the House of Representatives. This statement, like the Virginia resolution, does not merely challenge the correctness or wisdom of the Court's decision, but seems to deny the authority of the Court to render the decision. The Manifesto declares that the Supreme Court, without legal basis for its action, "undertook to exercise their naked judicial power," and pledges its signers "to use all lawful means to bring about a reversal of this decision which is contrary to the Constitution. . . ." Thus to characterize the decision of the Supreme Court is absurd. It ignores, if it does not challenge, the constitutional development of more than a century and a half through the well-established process of judicial review. The decision may be characterized as wrong, improper, or unwise, but under the American theory of constitutional law it may not be characterized as unconstitutional.

From a legal point of view, these statements are of no effect and have no significance whatever. But for the fact that they, along with other more extreme declarations, symbolize the extent and intensity of the resistance to the Court's order, they might be dismissed as merely a dramatic show of bad temper. Not to be ignored, however, is the campaign of "massive resistance" that was launched by the political leadership of some of the affected areas. These leaders have made it clear that they will leave no stone unturned to circumvent, evade, and delay the application of the Court's ruling. Most ironically, these determined attempts to evade a unanimous decision of our highest constitutional authority are

[73] Sen. Jt. Res. No. 3, Senate Journal and Documents, Virginia, 1956.
[74] See the *New York Times*, March 12, 1956.

accompanied by loud protestations of "reliance on the Constitution as the fundamental law of the land."

The Manifesto commendably urges that Southerners "scrupulously refrain from disorder and lawless acts," but the intemperate language of other parts of the declaration is not calculated to curb disorder and lawlessness.

It is clearly impossible to review here all the complex developments since the 1955 implementing decision, in connection with the application, or lack of application, of the Court's ruling. Suffice it to say that, since the decision that racial discrimination in public education is unconstitutional, the first step toward desegregation has not yet been taken in Virginia and several states of the deep South. On the contrary, consideration of the decision in these states looks solely toward prevention of its application.

However, the Supreme Court in its decision of September 12, 1958,[75] and in its opinion of September 29, 1958, makes it unmistakably clear that no scheme of racial discrimination against Negro children in attending schools can stand the test of the Fourteenth Amendment, if "there is state participation through any arrangement, management, funds or property." Furthermore, delay in carrying out the Court's desegregation ruling for the purpose of denying "the constitutional rights of Negro children" cannot be countenanced. Thus the entire body of state legislation enacted for the purpose of circumventing, evading, or delaying the application of the Court's decision would seem to be doomed. This is not to say that there will be widespread desegregation in the South in the near future. With every school district a potential battleground, prolonged litigation may be expected. Nevertheless, the movement of "massive resistance" against the Court's decision cannot but be defeated unless the people in the affected areas are willing to see their public schools destroyed. Thus the issue is now sharply drawn—the only alternative to some measure of desegregation is the complete elimination of the public school system by the state. Certain schools have already been closed in Little Rock, Ark., and in several communities in Virginia, but this action seems to be a clear denial of equal protection of the

[75] *Aaron v. Cooper,* 78 S. Ct. 1397 (1958).

laws, and in any event it is unthinkable that these schools will remain closed.

Finally, it should be noted that extremism is not confined to one side of this important issue. There are extremists among those who would comply with the Court's order, in that they would do the near-impossible before undertaking the relatively easy task. The fact that this group has greater provocation for extremism renders their action no less unwise. The extremists who would defy or nullify the Court's decision and those on the other side, who insist on starting desegregation in areas where it is most difficult, rather than where it would be relatively easy, alike do ill service both to the cause of public education and to the cause of constitutional government. Neither form of extremism appears to be in accordance with the spirit of the Court's implementing decision.

SUMMARY ANALYSIS

There can be little question that the most substantial contribution of the Supreme Court to the constitutional law of civil liberties since 1937 has been with respect to the political and social equality of the Negro. A significant landmark in the history of the South was the decision of the Court in *Smith* v. *Allwright,* by which the white primary was outlawed in state as well as national elections. This case, together with those which followed it for a decade, wrought a mild revolution in the political freedom of the Negro. The most ingenious devices for circumventing the Court's ruling against the white primary were struck down by the federal courts.

The controlling issue in all these cases, as in other race discrimination cases, was whether the action taken against the Negro was state action. In the principal case the Court declared that the constitutional right to be free from racial discrimination in voting cannot be nullified indirectly by a state, through casting its electoral process in a form permitting a private organization to practice racial discrimination in an election. The principle of the cases is that no election machinery can be sustained if its purpose or effect is to deny to the Negro, because of his race, an effective voice in the selection of his public officials or in the governmental affairs of his community or nation. Thus a state cannot escape the responsibility for unconstitutional discrimination, by delegating power to accomplish this purpose to a private organization or by taking any action which permits a private organization to accomplish such a purpose. The state may not become actively identified with nor materially aid a private scheme of racial discrimination.

Other subterfuges, such as grandfather clauses and restrictive registration requirements, have likewise been struck down by the Court as violative of the Fifteenth Amendment in purpose and effect. The suffrage cases as a whole seem to leave no legal loophole through which Negroes may be deprived of the ballot because of their race.

There remains, of course, the poll tax in five Southern states, and there seems little chance of eliminating this restriction on a national scale. The Court has sustained the tax as a qualification the states may impose for the exercise of the suffrage by national electors, and there is serious doubt that any act of Congress outlawing the poll tax would be sustained. This tax, however, is not as serious a restriction as it once was, for it is difficult to administer it so as to bar Negroes alone from the ballot box. Any administrative procedure by which the tax were to be exacted from the Negro alone would most certainly be invalidated by the federal courts.

Judicial condemnation of racial discrimination with respect to enjoyment of such social advantages as the occupancy and conveyance of real estate, the use of public transportation facilities, and educational opportunity has been no less impressive than that concerning political discrimination. A blow against private racial discrimination was struck by the Court in a series of restrictive covenant cases, in which it was held that state courts may not enforce private contracts involving racial discrimination in the acquisition, occupancy, and disposition of real estate. Intervention by the state courts makes the state a party to the discrimination in violation of the equal protection of the laws.

Segregation in public transportation had been largely eliminated as violative of the commerce clause of the Constitution or of the Interstate Commerce Act before the first *Brown* v. *Board* was decided. Since then, on the theory enunciated in that case, segregation in intrastate transportation, as well as on public golf courses and beaches, and in public parks and playgrounds, has been held violative of equal protection of the laws.

But the most significant as well as the most controversial case, not only of the period covered by this study but of the present century, is the school segregation case of *Brown* v. *Board of Education* referred to above. Here, the Court ordered removal of the public stigma of inferior status because of race, but the leeway allowed by the Court for compliance with its order apparently prompted widespread efforts looking toward indefinite evasion and defiance of the desegregation order. A decade or even a generation of prolific litigation of the matter may be expected.

The "Cold War" and
6 — Internal Security: I

When we come to know and understand our basic liberties, we recognize that they are not eternal and absolute truths, which must exist in equal degree in any and all circumstances. Even in ordinary times, they are necessarily limited by the equal rights of others and the general interests of the community. In time of war or threat of war, the demands of national safety place exceptionally serious strains on our civil liberties. If we needed any schooling to help us realize this, the two world wars of this century have taught it to us. We have learned that the exigencies of warfare make it necessary to prevent people from saying and doing many things which would be regarded as harmless, if not proper, in time of peace. As Mr. Justice Holmes remarked in the aforementioned Schenck case, "When a nation is at war many things that might be said in time of peace are such a hindrance to its effort that their utterance will not be endured so long as men fight and that no Court could regard them as protected by any constitutional right."

BASIC FREEDOMS

Yet, with the glaring exception of the Korematsu case[1] (which sustained, on the ground of military necessity, a military order under which 70,000 native-born Japanese-Americans were forced to leave their homes and occupations on the West Coast and spend the duration of the war in "war relocation centers" in the desert areas of the Far West), the Court's decisions during World War

[1] *Korematsu* v. *United States,* 323 U.S. 214 (1944).

II were generally favorable to the liberties of the individual. This attitude is illustrated by the decision in *Hartzel* v. *United States*,[2] also decided during the war. Like Schenck in 1919, Hartzel was convicted for violating the Espionage Act of 1917, and his offense was not substantially different from that of his earlier counterpart. However, the Court held the government to stricter standards of proof; it held that Hartzel's pamphlets opposing our war with Germany and defending German policies did not constitute a clear and present danger to our national security and, therefore, reversed his conviction.

With the emergence of the situation between the United States and the Kremlin, designated as the "cold war," about 1946, the judicial attitude of the Court changed in respect of basic liberties vis-à-vis subversion. The decade that followed was marked by suspicion, uncertainty, secrecy, fear, and hysteria on the part of a large segment of the American people. As a result of these disabling emotions and the incapacities they generated, our basic civil liberties faced threats and suffered setbacks probably as serious as at any time in our history. The fear, of course, was not altogether groundless. The external physical threat of nuclear war, with the possibility of total destruction, was made more clearly manifest by Communist infiltration into the industry and government of countries not under the control of the Kremlin. In addition, but with perhaps less reason, we have been fearful of the growth of communism in the United States.

Some of the attitudes toward these dangers and the methods of combating them in turn created other dangers and threats to the security of our basic civil liberties. Thus we faced a conflict "between physical security and the intangibles of our democratic principles the preservation of which are equally necessary to the safety of our nation."[3]

Certainly no thoughtful citizen would deny that military and industrial information and equipment must be protected from espionage and sabotage and that persons in our midst who are committed to furthering the revolutionary objectives of a foreign

[2] 322 U.S. 680 (1944).
[3] Eleanor Bontecou, "Does the Loyalty Program Threaten Civil Rights?" *The Annals*, Vol. 275 (May, 1951), p. 118.

power should be barred from positions of influence and power in the government. It is, however, equally important that, in the process, our basic liberties not be destroyed or seriously impaired. Otherwise a program for the control of subversion will become self-defeating. The highest purpose of national security is to preserve individual freedom.

Of course, the initiative in the control of subversion is taken by the legislative and executive branches of the government. Our concern here is with the Court's response to these programs. For this purpose, we limit the discussion to the Court's response to (1) federal antisubversive legislation, (2) the loyalty and security programs, (3) the application of subversive control programs to aliens and naturalized citizens, and (4) the legislative investigatory power. The first of these will be discussed in the next chapter.

THE COURT'S RESPONSE TO ANTISUBVERSION PROGRAMS

Executive Loyalty and Security Programs

On the national level, one answer to the problem of Communist subversion was the institution of an elaborate system for the investigation and screening of public employees. As Justice Jackson observed, "The Government is using its power as never before to pry into their lives and thoughts upon the slightest suspicion of less than complete trustworthiness."[4] The President's Loyalty Order of March 21, 1947, set up an elaborate scheme to rid the Executive branch of the government of disloyal employees. It required an investigation into the loyalty not only of every person entering the government, but also of those already in the government. The order fixed a standard for determining the loyalty of employees and provided procedures by which employees, charged with disloyalty and recommended for dismissal by the Loyalty Board of their respective departments or agencies, could have their cases reviewed by a Central Loyalty Review Board in the Civil Service Commission. The standard for removal prescribed by the order was whether,

[4] Dissenting opinion in *Frazier* v. *United States,* 335 U.S. 497 (1948).

On all the evidence, reasonable grounds exist for the belief that the person involved is disloyal to the Government of the United States. [The standard of judgment was revised in 1951 to read:] On all the evidence there is a reasonable doubt as to the loyalty of the person involved to the Government of the United States.[5]

Although this standard seems fair and reasonable on its face, its omissions may seriously endanger civil liberties. The employee is not entitled to know who his accusers are or to confront or cross-examine them. He is, therefore, unable to defend himself against malicious gossip or idle rumor. In the words of Justice Douglas, the critical evidence may be the word of an unknown witness who "is a paragon of veracity, a knave, or the village idiot!" Equally serious is a provision of the order authorizing the Attorney General to draw up a list of organizations which he finds to be

totalitarian fascist, communist or subversive or as having adopted a policy of advocating or approving the commission of acts of force or violence to deny others their rights under the Constitution of the United States, or as seeking to alter the form of government of the United States by unconstitutional means.

In determining a person's loyalty, investigators are directed to consider his membership in, affiliation with, or sympathetic association with organizations thus designated by the Attorney General.

The later Eisenhower loyalty-security program in one respect carries a greater hazard than the Truman program, in that it provides for reopening the cases of all persons in the government whose files contain derogatory information, even though they had received clearance under the earlier program. Considering the diversity of materials and data collected by the F.B.I. from every conceivable source, and of every degree of credibility and incredibility in line with its duty, employees may well be placed in perpetual jeopardy. The names of Condon, Davies, and Oppenheimer, not to mention countless lesser lights whose names never become the subject of public controversy, suggest the possibilities of this phase of the later program.

The conflicting views concerning the constitutionality of this program came before the Supreme Court in three cases, but with

[5] Executive Order 10,241, 16 Fed. Reg. 3590.

inconclusive and unsatisfactory results. In *Bailey* v. *Richardson*,[6] the loyalty order was sustained by an evenly divided Court (Justice Clark not participating), against claims of unconstitutionality on due process and First Amendment grounds. The government had been sustained in the Court of Appeals by a 2 to 1 vote, and the even division of the Supreme Court, of course, affirmed this decision without opinion. In this case a finding of disloyalty was made against Dorothy Bailey, and she was dismissed from her government position on the basis of unsworn reports, based on the unsworn statements of unknown informants. Miss Bailey denied all charges except past membership in one organization listed by the Attorney General. Although she had no power to subpoena witnesses, four appeared on her behalf and others submitted some seventy affidavits. All the evidence of witnesses was in her favor, and no affidavits were introduced against her.

In announcing the decision of the Court of Appeals,[7] Judge Prettyman stated that Miss Bailey's case is "undoubtedly appealing" because "she was not given a trial in any sense of the word, and she does not know who informed upon her." Nor indeed did the Loyalty Review Board have "the slightest knowledge" about her accusers. However, continued Judge Prettyman, "it so happens that we are presently in an adversary position to a government whose most successful recent method of contest is the infiltration of a government service by its sympathizers." It might be added that we are in that adversary position because we believe in the value of personal freedom and in its preservation.

All objections to the dismissal and the methods by which it was effected were brushed aside, including free speech objections, concerning which the Court asserted that the First Amendment does not guarantee government employment. Dismissal of government employees on loyalty-security grounds seems, then, to be no different legally from dismissal on other grounds. This conclusion is rooted in the assumption, well supported by precedent, that no one has a right to public employment and that removal or disqualification is not punishment. The President, in the ab-

6 341 U.S. 918 (1951).
7 182 F. 2d. 46 (1950).

sence of Congressional limitation in certain areas, is free to remove any employee of the government without notice or assigned reason.

Yet, this case could have been decided on the basis of *United States* v. *Lovett*,[8] in which the Supreme Court held invalid as a bill of attainder the provision of a deficiency appropriation act, forbidding the payment of salaries of three designated federal employees from funds carried in the act. A bill of attainder is "a legislative act which inflicts punishment without a judicial trial," and Justice Black declared for the Court in Lovett that "permanent proscription from any opportunity to serve the Government is punishment, and of a most severe type."

The Court did, however, strike down the irregular manner in which the Attorney General made up his list of subversive organizations without a hearing. In 1949 the Joint Anti-Fascist Refugee Committee, along with certain other organizations, sought to restrain the Attorney General from including its name in a list of organizations designated by him to be subversive. The Supreme Court by a 5 to 3 vote reversed holdings of the courts below which had denied relief.[9] So great was the diversity of opinion among the majority that it is difficult to determine what the effect of the judgment is. Justice Burton who announced the judgment of the Court (there was no opinion for the Court as such) took the view, supported by Justice Douglas, that the Attorney General's listing of the complainants was not authorized by the President's Executive Order 9835, which sets forth the procedure for determining the loyalty of federal employees or prospective employees. Justice Black insisted that the Attorney General had violated the First Amendment and that the President's order constituted a bill of attainder. He, along with Justices Frankfurter, Jackson, and Douglas, also held that the Attorney General had deprived the petitioners of due process of law by failing to give them notice and hearing.

There was reason to hope that the uncertain constitutional situation with respect to the loyalty-security program would be resolved when the Supreme Court agreed to review the Peters

[8] 328 U.S. 303 (1946).
[9] *Joint Anti-Fascist Refugee Committee* v. *McGrath*, 341 U.S. 123 (1951).

case.[10] This hope was dissipated by the Court's refusal to face up to the serious constitutional issues presented by the case. Instead, it decided the case in Dr. Peters' favor on a narrow procedural point—that the Loyalty Review Board in reviewing a former decision of the agency board on its own motion had violated the executive order of the President. The Review Board was limited to cases involving persons recommended for dismissal by the Loyalty Board of the department or agency of the employee, and referred to it by such department or agency.

This decision is the more surprising and disappointing since the Court had granted certiorari "because the case appeared to present the same constitutional question left unresolved by the Court's action" in the Bailey case, and also since Dr. Peters had urged the Court to decide the case solely on the constitutional issue.

On the constitutional question, Peters' chief complaints were: (1) that the denial of an opportunity to confront and cross-examine his secret accusers, and his removal and debarment from the government service on their unsworn testimony, deprived him of liberty and property without due process of law; (2) that rendering him ineligible for government service constituted imposition of a penalty without a fair trial and was, therefore, a bill of attainder; and (3) that his removal and debarment from government service, solely on the basis of his political opinions, denied his right to freedom of speech.

The Court, however, took refuge in a long-established judicial rule that it will not decide a question of constitutional law until it is necessary to do so. Thus, left unresolved were the vital constitutional issues presented by the Bailey case four years before, apparently because: "This issue, if reached by the Court, would obviously present serious and far-reaching problems in reconciling fundamental constitutional guarantees with the procedures used to determine the loyalty of government personnel." It would appear that the majority hoped to ride out the "cold war" before coming to grips with these issues.

Justice Douglas, in a concurring opinion, thought the Court could not avoid the constitutional issue. He said:

[10] *Peters* v. *Hobby*, 349 U.S. 331 (1955).

We have here a system where government with all its power and authority condemns a man to a suspect class and the outer darkness, without the rudiments of a fair trial. When we relax our standards to accommodate the faceless informer, we violate our basic constitutional guarantees and ape the tactics of those whom we despise.

In 1956, the Court, by means of narrow statutory construction, limited the scope of the federal employee fidelity program, again without deciding any of the serious constitutional questions posed in the litigation. In *Cole* v. *Young*,[11] the summary suspension powers of department heads under the Summary Suspension Act of 1950 were held to apply only to those employees who worked "in sensitive positions." The act gives the heads of eleven designated departments and agencies powers of summary suspension and unreviewable dismissal of their civilian employees, when deemed necessary "in the interest of national security." In pursuance of Sec. 3 of the act, providing that it would be extended "to such other departments and agencies of the Government as the President may deem necessary in the best interest of national security," the President, by executive order, extended the act to all other departments and agencies of the government. Cole, a preference-eligible veteran under the Veteran's Preference Act, was summarily suspended from his classified civil service position as a food and drug inspector in the Department of Health, Education and Welfare, on charges of association with alleged Communists and of sympathetic association with an alleged subversive organization. Later he was dismissed, on the ground that his continued employment was not "clearly consistent with the interests of national security." His appeal to the Civil Service Commission under the Veteran's Act was denied, on the ground that the act was not applicable to such discharges.

By a 6 to 3 vote, the Court held that Cole's dismissal was not authorized by the Summary Suspension Act and hence violated the Veteran's Preference Act. The Court construed the dismissal procedure of the 1950 act as applicable only if the discharge is in the "interest of national security" and defined this term as relating only to employees' activities "which are directly concerned with the Nation's safety." In arriving at this definition, the Court

[11] 351 U.S. 536 (1956).

was influenced by the type of agency to which Congress had specifically granted summary suspension and nonappealable dismissal powers. Since all these agencies were closely connected with the national defense, the inference seems to have been drawn that the President's power to extend the coverage of the act was limited to the so-called sensitive agencies.

It should be noted that the decision in this case in no way limits the substantive power of the government to provide for the dismissal of employees on loyalty grounds. It simply holds that the summary procedures authorized by the act are not applicable in a situation unrelated to the national safety.

This case may signify a different pattern for future cases of this type, but it has not yet been judicially conceded that public employees under loyalty investigation have a constitutional right to confrontation, cross examination, and judicial hearing. The loyalty procedure guarantees them notice, charges, and freedom from summary suspension and nonreviewable dismissal except "in sensitive positions," and they are entitled to no more.

State Loyalty Oaths

The favorite method of the states for combating Communist subversion among employees during the "cold war" has been the requirement of a loyalty oath and non-Communist affidavits. Of the state statutory requirements of a loyalty oath that have come before the Supreme Court, only one has been held invalid, and this not because of any lack of power to require a loyalty oath as such. In *Garner* v. *Board of Public Works*[12] in 1951, the Court upheld a Los Angeles ordinance, barring from city employment any person who would not take an oath swearing that he does not and has not for five years past advised, advocated, or taught the violent overthrow of the government; that he is not, and has not been, a member of any group advocating such activity; and that he will not engage in such forbidden activities while in the employment of the city. The Court also upheld the requirement of non-Communist affidavits required of all city employees.

Seven of the nine justices held that a revelation of party membership was a reasonable requirement, relating to the establishment

12 341 U.S. 716 (1951).

of qualifications for public office. On the loyalty oath requirement, which in terms made no distinction between knowing and unknowing membership in a subversive organization, the Court divided 5 to 4. The majority, through Justice Clark, upheld the loyalty oath in the belief that *scienter* was implicit in the ordinance and on the assumption that California courts would not so construe the oath as to include innocent membership in subversive organizations. In an earlier case [13] the Court, upholding a part of the Ober Act of Maryland, which required candidates for public office to sign an oath that they are not engaged in any manner in attempting to overthrow the government and that they are not members of any organization engaged in such activity, had stressed that its decision was based on the assumption that what was forbidden was the overthrow of the government by force or violence. Although the Court sustained the loyalty oath in both these cases, it agreed that the doctrine of guilt by association could be carried to the point of denying due process of law.

A year later, however, in *Adler* v. *Board of Education*,[14] Mr. Justice Minton placed the stamp of the Court's approval upon this doctrine. In this case the Court sustained the Civil Service Law of New York, as implemented by the Feinberg Law of 1949. The first denies public employment to persons who willfully advocate or teach the overthrow of government by any unlawful means or who join any group advocating such a policy. The Feinberg Law requires the Board of Regents of the state "after inquiry, and after such notice and hearing as may be appropriate," to prepare a list of subversive organizations to be used, along with similar listing of any federal agency, in removing and barring from the public schools ineligible employees. Membership in any listed organization is *prima facie* evidence of disqualification for employment in the public schools.

After pointing out that listings are made only after full notice and hearing, and that the New York Court of Appeals had ruled that the listed organizations have the right of appeal, the Court held that the Feinberg Law did not violate free speech and free assembly of persons employed or seeking employment in the public

---

[13] *Gerende* v. *Board of Supervisors of Elections,* 341 U.S. 56 (1951).
[14] 342 U.S. 485 (1952).

schools. It is clear, said Mr. Justice Minton, that such persons have the right to "assemble, speak, think and believe as they will, but it is equally clear that they have no right to employment in the school system on their own terms." If they do not choose to work under "the reasonable terms laid down by the proper authorities," they are "free to retain their beliefs and associations and go elsewhere."

With respect to guilt by association, Mr. Justice Minton said for the majority: "One's associates, past and present, as well as one's conduct, may properly be considered in determining fitness and loyalty. From time immemorial, one's reputation has been determined in part by the company he keeps."

Justice Douglas, with Justice Black agreeing, was unable to "accept the recent doctrine" that public servants may be constitutionally placed "in the category of second class citizens by denying them freedom of thought and expression." The procedure allowed by this law "is certain to raise havoc with academic freedom," said Douglas. Furthermore this law "turns the school system into a spying project." Once membership is established, the view of the teacher must be examined to determine whether his affiliation was or is innocent. Douglas declared:

There can be no academic freedom in such an environment. Where suspicion fills the air and holds scholars in line for fear of their jobs, there can be no exercise of the free intellect. . . . A problem can no longer be pursued with impunity to its edges. Fear stalks the classroom. The teacher is no longer a stimulant to adventurous thinking; she becomes instead a pipeline for safe and sound information. A deadening dogma takes the place of free inquiry. Instruction tends to become sterile; pursuit of knowledge is discouraged; discussion often leaves off where it should begin.

Perhaps Justice Douglas' apprehensions were somewhat relieved by the unanimous decision of the Court the following term in *Weiman* v. *Updegraff*.[15] In this case the Court condemned guilt by association and held unconstitutional, on due process grounds, the Oklahoma loyalty oath act because, as applied to a member of the faculty of Oklahoma A. & M. College, it excluded people from state employment solely on the basis of membership in organiza-

---

[15] 344 U.S. 183 (1952).

tions listed by the Attorney General of the United States as "Communist front" or "subversive." Justice Clark, for the Court, points out that in previous loyalty oath cases the Court had made its decision on the understanding that knowing membership in the proscribed organization was an implicit requirement of the statute. Under the Oklahoma law as interpreted by the state court, knowledge was not a factor. Hence mere membership is made a conclusive presumption of disloyalty.

"But membership may be innocent. A state servant may have joined a proscribed organization unaware of its activities and purposes." Such indiscriminate classification of innocent with knowing affiliation is, therefore, condemned "as an assertion of arbitrary power" in violation of due process.

Although this case apparently placed the preceding loyalty oath cases in a less disturbing light from the point of view of the public employee, it in no way challenged the power of the states to impose loyalty tests upon their employees. It merely held this particular loyalty test bad for the reasons indicated. Still, it was encouraging to public servants to have the Court deny that the unfortunate language of Mr. Justice Minton in the Adler case supports the conclusion "that there is no constitutionally protected right to public employment." Declining to consider whether there is an abstract right to public employment, the Court nevertheless emphasized "that constitutional protection does extend to the public servant whose exclusion pursuant to a statute is patently arbitrary and discriminatory."

The Privilege Against Self-Incrimination

A less common method of insuring the loyalty of state and local employees is illustrated by the provision of the Charter of the City of New York, which stipulates that whenever any employee of the city invokes the privilege against self-incrimination for the purpose of avoiding disclosure of information relating to his official conduct, he shall be automatically discharged and rendered ineligible for future employment. In *Slochower* v. *Board of Education*,[16] a professor at Brooklyn College was automatically discharged for having pleaded self-incrimination before a U. S. Senate investigat-

[16] 350 U.S. 551 (1956).

ing committee with respect to Communist membership and association prior to 1941. Slochower testified that he was not a member of the Communist Party and that he was willing to answer all questions relating to such membership subsequent to 1941, but he refused to answer questions about his membership during 1940–41 for fear of self-incrimination.

The Supreme Court, reversing the Court of Appeals of New York, held that Slochower's summary dismissal without charges, notice, hearing, and the right of appeal denied him due process of law.

Although the majority opinion is something less than clear as to which aspects of the discharge procedure failed to satisfy due process requirements, the holding of invalidity seems to rest upon two related considerations: First, under the Charter provision a claim of the privilege against self-incrimination creates a conclusive presumption of unsuitability for employment. Second, a provision that bars any weighing of the circumstances in which the privilege was claimed is arbitrary on its face. This point was emphasized by the majority of five.

It should be noted, then, that the Court did not rule that the plea of self-incrimination by an employee could not be made valid ground for dismissal; it held rather that Slochower was entitled to a fair hearing to determine whether in the circumstances of his case such a plea was a proper ground for dismissal.

The principal significance of the Slochower case is its reaffirmation of the proposition of the Wieman case, that "constitutional protection does extend to the public servant whose exclusion pursuant to a statute is patently arbitrary and discriminatory." The decision also refutes the dictum of the Bailey case that public employment is a "privilege" which escapes protection entirely.

State Legislative Investigation

The case of *Sweezy* v. *New Hampshire*,[17] which will be considered later in connection with Congressional powers of investigation, further limited the power of the states to encroach upon the rights of public employees in their search for subversives. The legislature of New Hampshire had in 1951 enacted a comprehen-

[17] 354 U.S. 234 (1957).

sive Subversive Activities Act and in 1953 authorized and directed the Attorney General of the state to make full and complete investigation of subversive activities and persons. He was authorized to act on his own motion upon such information as in his judgment was reasonable and reliable, and was given the further authority to subpoena witnesses and documents. Although he did not have power to hold witnesses in contempt, he could invoke the aid of a state Superior Court for this purpose.

Sweezy, a university professor, was summoned to testify before the Attorney General. Although he had previously testified that he had never been a member of the Communist Party, that he had no knowledge of any violations of the Subversive Activities Act or of the presence of subversive persons within the state, he refused to answer, both before the Attorney General and before the Superior Court, questions relating to the content of a lecture he had delivered at the University of New Hampshire and questions concerning his and others' association with the Progressive Party. His refusal to answer those questions was based on his contention that they were not pertinent to the subject of the inquiry and that they infringed upon an area protected by the First and Fourteenth Amendments. For this refusal to answer, Sweezy was held guilty of contempt. The Supreme Court reversed the conviction on the ground that it had denied the defendant due process of law.

The meaning of this decision is not unmistakably clear because of the division in the opinion of the six majority justices. Four justices (Warren, Black, Douglas, and Brennan), although placing great emphasis on the infringement of Sweezy's academic freedom and his right of political association, seemed to hold that the conviction was bad because the legislature, in its sweeping grant of discretionary authority to the Attorney General, had divested itself of all responsibility for the direction of the investigation. So broad and uncertain is the mandate of the Attorney General that the matters to be investigated, the witnesses to be summoned, and the questions to be asked are all left to his discretion. "In this circumstance," said the Chief Justice, "it cannot be determined authoritatively that the legislature asked the attorney general to gather the kind of facts comprised in the subjects upon which petitioner was interrogated." Justices Frankfurter and Harlan agreed that the conviction should be set aside, but on the ground that the questions asked of Sweezy deprived him of his constitutionally protected rights of academic freedom and political association.

Although the precise manner in which the Fourteenth Amendment was violated does not emerge clearly from the divided opinions of the justices, all six members of the majority seem to agree that the academic freedom of a university teacher and the political freedom of a citizen are constitutionally protected against the state investigatory power through the due process clause of the Fourteenth Amendment, unless the state can show a very strong countervailing interest.

Deportation of Aliens and Denaturalization of Citizens

Where subversive control programs have related to aliens or to naturalized citizens, the Court has been especially reluctant to intervene in behalf of individual freedoms. The complete power of Congress over the admission of aliens to this country and the responsibility of the Executive for the conduct of foreign affairs make it easy for the Court to maintain a role of passivity with respect to subversive control relating to aliens. The virtually absolute power of Congress to prescribe the standards for admission of aliens into the United States has been well established for more than a half-century,[18] and with this power goes also a broad control of aliens after their admission to the country. By the Alien Registration Act of 1940, for example, it was provided that all aliens fourteen years of age and over, residing in the United States, submit to registration and fingerprinting. Failure to comply was made a criminal offense against the United States.[19] Should he, while residing in the United States, violate the rules and regulations laid down by Congress for the control of his conduct, the alien may be deported.

The attitude of judicial restraint on the part of the Court in alien cases became much more pronounced in the postwar period than during World War II. In the earlier period it had been held,

[18] See *Turner* v. *Williams*, 194 U.S. 279 (1904).
[19] 54 Stat. 670, 673.

for example, that Communist belief and affiliation which had ceased at the time of the defendant's arrest was not a proper ground for deportation under the Immigration Act of 1918.[20] Furthermore, co-operation with the Communist Party in lawful activities did not constitute affiliation within the meaning of the Alien Registration Act of 1940, which authorized the deportation of any alien affiliated with an organization believing in or advocating the overthrow of the government by force or violence.[21]

On the other hand, in 1952, a provision of the Internal Security Act of 1950, authorizing the Attorney General, in his discretion, to hold in custody without bail alien Communists pending determination of their deportability was sustained by the Court in a 5 to 4 vote.[22] The Court had no doubt of the validity of the provision of the law making membership in the Communist Party alone a cause for deportation, for "so long as aliens fail to become and remain naturalized citizens, they remain subject to the plenary power of Congress to expel them under the sovereign right to determine what non-citizens shall be permitted to remain within our borders." Detention, even for life, was held to be a necessary part of deportation procedure.

Justice Black, in dissent, thought that condemning people to jail was a job for the judiciary, not the Attorney General, and that to keep people in jail because of what they said was a clear violation of the First Amendment.

On the same day, the Court, with only Douglas and Black dissenting, sustained a provision of the Alien Registration Act of 1940, authorizing the deportation of legally resident aliens on account of membership in the Communist Party, which terminated before the enactment of the act. The Court in *Harisiades* v. *Shaughnessy*[23] held that such deportation did not deprive the alien petitioners of liberty without due process of law, even though it might be unreasonably and harshly exercised under this statute, (1) because the power to expel aliens is a weapon of defense and reprisal, confirmed by international law as a power inherent in

---

[20] *Kessler* v. *Strecher,* 357 U.S. 22 (1939).
[21] *Bridges* v. *Wixon,* 326 U.S. 135 (1945).
[22] *Carlson* v. *Landon,* 342 U.S. 524 (1952).
[23] 342 U.S. 580 (1952).

every sovereign state; (2) because the policy toward aliens is so exclusively entrusted to the political branches of the government as to be largely immune from judicial inquiry or interference. As Justice Frankfurter observed in a concurring opinion, "the place to resist unwise or cruel legislation touching aliens is the Congress, not this Court."

The Court also held that the act did not abridge the aliens' rights of free speech and free assembly in contravention of the First Amendment. Under the First Amendment, said Justice Jackson for the majority, Congress may make a distinction between advocacy of change by lawful elective processes and change by force and violence.

In 1954, in *Galvan* v. *Press*,[24] the Court held that an alien was deportable even if he had no knowledge of the illegal purposes of the Communist Party.

In a case decided in 1957, a point is scored in favor of the alien, in a holding that the Attorney General is forbidden to ask an alien, under order of deportation, questions that do not relate to his availability for expulsion.[25]

In the present state of the law, as reflected in the cases of the 1950's, it is not easy to say what rights, if any, aliens have when threatened with deportation. It has long been well established that they are "persons" within the meaning of the due process clause of the Fifth Amendment, but they cease to have the rights of native persons when deportation threatens.

Even naturalized citizens are subject to serious disabilities when the question of defense against charges of subversion arises. Chief Justice Marshall asserted, in 1824, that a naturalized citizen becomes a full-fledged member of the society into which he is admitted, "possessing all the rights of a native citizen, and standing, in the view of the Constitution, on the footing of a native. The Constitution does not authorize Congress to enlarge or abridge those rights"[26] other than to prescribe a uniform rule of naturalization. Justice Douglas expressed a similar view for the Court in 1946:

[24] 347 U.S. 522 (1954).
[25] *United States* v. *Witkovick*, 353 U.S. 194 (1957).
[26] *Osborn* v. *Bank of United States*, 9 Wheat 738, 827 (1824).

Citizenship obtained through naturalization is not second class citizenship. . . . [It] carried with it the privilege of full participation in the affairs of our society, including the right to speak freely, to criticize officials and administrators, and to promote changes in our laws including the very charter of our government.[27]

Nevertheless, the device of denaturalization can and has been used against naturalized citizens who express unorthodox political views.[28] The power to denaturalize is, of course, implied from the power of Congress to provide a uniform rule of naturalization and is based on the charge that naturalization was obtained through fraud or illegality. There has never been any question of the legality of canceling certificates of naturalization thus obtained. If it can be shown that the applicant has sworn falsely that he was "attached to the principles of the United States, and well disposed to the good order and happiness of the same," his certificate may be canceled. In determining the standards of proof that must be observed to support the government's charges in such cases, the courts enlarge or contract the civil liberties of naturalized citizens. Enlargement was achieved in some denaturalization cases of World War II, the leading one being *Schneiderman* v. *United States*.[29]

Here, the Court held that before the citizenship of a naturalized citizen could be canceled, the government must present evidence of his failure to meet the statutory requirements of attachment to the principles of the Constitution that is "clear, unequivocal, and convincing." A mere preponderance of evidence is not enough. The government had failed to meet this standard of proof in its case against Schneiderman, and the denaturalization decree of the lower court was set aside. Because of our firmly rooted tradition of freedom of belief, the Court in construing the denaturalization acts refused to presume "that Congress meant to circumscribe liberty of political thought by general phrases in those statutes."[30]

Here, the Court had required a burden of proof of the government in denaturalization cases which in effect approximates the

27 *Knauer* v. *United States*, 328 U.S. 654, 658 (1946).
28 See C. H. Pritchett, *Civil Liberties and the Vinson Court* (Chicago, University of Chicago Press, 1954), p. 103.
29 320 U.S. 118 (1943).
30 See also *Baumgartner* v. *United States*, 322 U.S. 665 (1944).

burden demanded for conviction in criminal cases, namely, proof beyond a reasonable doubt of the charges alleged. Yet, five years after Baumgartner, in 1949, the Court ruled in *Klaprott* v. *United States* [31] that the strict procedural standards of a criminal trial need not be observed in denaturalization cases. It should be added, however, that cases decided in 1956 and 1957 may mark reversion of the Court to a more favorable attitude to the citizen. For example, in *United States* v. *Miniker* [32] it was held that the provision of the Immigration and Nationality Act of 1952, relating to the compulsion of testimony in deportation and denaturalization proceedings, does not empower an immigration officer to subpoena a naturalized citizen to testify in an administrative proceeding in which determination of his denaturalization is the subject of the investigation.

Legislative Investigatory Power

The legislative response to the Communist menace that has provoked perhaps the sharpest controversy in the postwar years took the form of the legislative investigatory power. There can be no question, of course, that few things should be of greater concern to Congress than the security of the nation and its protection against subversion and conspiracy. But of equal importance is protection of the rights of the individual against possible abuses of the investigatory power. Since 1937, there have been many complaints that some legislative committees were guilty of such abuses.

On the basis of well-established precedents, it is clear that the courts can exercise no substantial restraint upon the exercise of this legislative function. Investigative powers are, of course, not specifically stated in the Constitution but are derived by implication from the delegated powers of Congress as incidental to the effective exercise of those powers. Until the Watkins case, there had actually been only one case [33] in which the Supreme Court failed to find relevance to the delegated powers of Congress.

It was nearly a century after the framing of the Constitution

[31] 335 U.S. 601 (1949).

[32] 350 U.S. 179 (1956); see also *United States* v. *Zucca*, 351 U.S. 90 (1957).

[33] See note 34.

before the first case to challenge the securing of information by compulsory legislative process reached the Supreme Court. In the case of *Kilbourne* v. *Thompson*,[34] in 1881, the Court held an investigation invalid because Congress was without power to legislate with respect to the subject of the investigation. The investigation involved an effort to pry into purely private affairs, with which the judiciary alone was empowered to deal, and hence violated the principle of the separation of powers. The Court also indicated that the investigating committee's authorizing resolution must recite a proper legislative purpose, but in *McGrain* v. *Daugherty*,[35] in 1927, the rule was enunciated that when the subject matter of the investigation is one from which valid legislation might ensue, a proper legislative purpose will be presumed, whether or not this were the actual situation. Here the Court declared "that the power of inquiry—with process to enforce it— is an essential and appropriate auxiliary to the legislative function."

Aided by the aforementioned presumption of regularity, and the consequent reluctance of courts to find in contempt proceedings that investigations were conducted for improper purposes, the committees have been able to carry on investigations aimed at exposure rather than at corrective legislation. For many years both the legislatures and the courts seem to have overlooked the qualifications of the McGrain case, namely, that the investigation must be in aid of a valid legislative function, and that the questions asked must be pertinent to the subject of the inquiry.

This broadening of the investigatory power assumed a form, in the post-World War II years, hitherto unknown. The investigations of this period were concerned almost exclusively with the problems of subversion, and they brought before the courts new questions of the appropriate limits of Congressional investigation. The central issue here was the application of the Bill of Rights as a restraint upon the assertion of the investigatory powers of Congress.

The activities of the House Committee on Un-American Activities were challenged in several cases, in 1947, on substantive

[34] 103 U.S. 168 (1881).
[35] 273 U.S. 135 (1927).

constitutional issues. The Supreme Court refused to review all but one of these cases, and in that one, the flight of the defendant from the country prevented the Court's rendering a decision on the merits of the controversy. In this and the four other cases, the constitutional issues were decided by the Court of Appeals in favor of the Committee.[36] With respect to the four cases finally determined by the Court of Appeals, the Supreme Court apparently saw no reason to question the holdings and reasoning of the lower courts. The fact that the Committee showed little, or no, interest in legislation made no difference to the Court of Appeals. It followed *McGrain* v. *Daugherty* in regarding the declaration by Congress that the information sought by it in creating the committee was for a legislative purpose as binding on the courts.

In these cases a new attack was made on the work of investigative committees by attempts to show that the results achieved by the Committee violated the First Amendment. For example, the argument of the appellant in the case of *United States* v. *Josephson*[37] ran substantially in this fashion: The Committee's power to investigate is limited by Congress' power to legislate; Congress is without power to legislate upon matters of thought and speech; therefore, a statute empowering a Congressional committee to investigate such matters is unconstitutional. One of the three judges of the Court of Appeals accepted this argument, but the response of the majority was that Congress clearly can and should legislate to curtail this freedom, where there is a clear and present danger that its exercise would imperil the safety of the country and its constitutional system, and that courts cannot anticipate that Congress will enact legislation in violation of the First Amendment.

The contention that the Committee's questioning of witnesses as to their political affiliation violated their First Amendment rights to privacy and to freedom from inquiry into political beliefs

---

[36] *United States* v. *Josephson,* 165 F. 2d. 82 (1947), cert. denied 333 U.S. 838 (1948); *Barsky* v. *United States,* 167 F. 2d. 241 (1948), cert. denied 334 U.S. 843 (1948); *Eisler* v. *United States,* 170 F. 2d. 273 (1948), cert. granted 335 U.S. 857 (1948); *Lawson* v. *United States,* 176 F. 2d. 49 (1949), cert. denied 339 U.S. 934 (1950); *Marshall* v. *United States,* 176 F. 2d. 473 (1949), cert. denied 339 U.S. 933.

[37] 165 F. 2d. 82 (1947).

was likewise rejected by the Court of Appeals. Such questioning is incidental to the Committee's principal function of securing information with a view to determining whether party affiliations or activities do in fact constitute a clear and present danger. In such circumstances the right to privacy must give way to the Congressional interest in safeguarding the public welfare. Rejected also was the argument that the authorization to the Committee to examine into "the extent, character, and objects of un-American propaganda activities in the United States" was so vague as to deny due process.

Apparently the Supreme Court at this time had no desire to become involved in the problem of determining the boundaries of legislative inquiry. At any rate, it had placed no restraint upon any committee investigating Communist activity. The Court did, however, rule against the House Select Committee on Lobbying in its attempt to secure information from the Secretary of the self-styled Committee on Constitutional Government with respect to the names of the purchasers of its propaganda materials in bulk. The Regulation of Lobbying Act of 1946 requires the reporting of all contributions of $500 or more received or expended for the purpose of influencing legislation. The Committee on Constitutional Government, commonly regarded as a right-wing propaganda organization, adopted the policy of accepting payments of over $490 only if the contributor specified that the money was to be used for the distribution of books and pamphlets. The organization described these practices as sales and hence refused to report them. The Committee on Lobbying responded to what it regarded as a transparent attempt at evasion of the law by citing the Secretary, Rumely, for contempt. In *United States* v. *Rumely*,[38] the Supreme Court unanimously reversed the conviction of Rumely for contempt, but the decision seemed to be of little value as a precedent, for only Douglas and Black were willing to face the constitutional issue of First Amendment violation. The Court evaded this issue, as indicated in Chapter 3, by holding that the Committee was authorized by Congress to investigate lobbying, that lobbying as defined in the statute means only the direct attempt to influence legislation and does not extend to general ef-

[38] 345 U.S. 41 (1953).

forts to influence the opinion of the community by the circulation of books and pamphlets.

Before the cases beginning in 1955, it appears then that the position of the Court on judicial review of the scope of the legislative investigatory function could be summed up in the statement of Justice Frankfurter, in *Tenney* v. *Brandhove*,[39] that to justify a judicial finding that a committee's investigation has exceeded the bounds of legislative power, "it must be obvious that there was a usurpation of functions exclusively vested in the executive or the courts."

However, a redefinition of the scope of legislative investigation was in the making, and even the charge of First Amendment violation made in the Josephson case[40] was destined to bear fruit. In a series of cases decided in the 1955 term, the Court recognized the privilege against self-incrimination as a legal limitation on the powers of Congressional investigating committees.

In three companion cases,[41] the Court faced the problem of recalcitrant witnesses before Congressional investigating committees. Each defendant had been convicted of contempt of Congress for refusing to answer questions put to them by a subcommittee of the House Committee on Un-American Activities. The Court in three opinions by Chief Justice Warren reversed the convictions.

The controlling issues, as framed by the Court were: (1) whether the defendants had invoked their constitutional privilege against self-incrimination with a sufficient degree of specificity (this issue was not involved in the Bart case); and (2) whether, assuming that they had not, the Committee had made its refusal to accept the defendant's objections sufficiently clear to support a finding that they had intended to defy the Committee's authority. Despite the fact that Quinn and Emspak had stated their reasons for refusal to answer in something less than unequivocal terms, the Chief Justice nevertheless declared that the responsibility for clarification of ambiguities in the witness' position rests on the interrogator. A valid claim of the privilege does not depend upon

[39] 341 U.S. 367, 378 (1951).
[40] See note 37, p. 138.
[41] *Quinn* v. *United States,* 349 U.S. 155 (1955); *Emspak* v. *United States,* 349 U.S. 190 (1955); *Bart* v. *United States,* 349 U.S. 219 (1955).

any special combination of words. Thus Emspak's refusal, based on "primarily the first Amendment, supplemented by the fifth," was sufficient. The Court pointed out that, in common parlance today, the Fifth Amendment is taken to mean privilege against self-incrimination. On the issue of criminal intent to defy the Committee, the Court ruled that the Committee had failed to make it sufficiently clear that it was not willingly abandoning those questions to which objection had been made. Thus the witness may have thought that his objections had been sustained. In short, there must be a clear disposition of the witness' objection before there can be a prosecution for contempt. The Committee's failure to rule on the objections was fatal to a citation for contempt.

Although it had previously been assumed that the privilege against self-incrimination could be invoked by witnesses called before Congressional investigating committees, the Supreme Court had not ruled on this question up to this point. These decisions, however, imposed no important substantive limitations on Congressional investigative procedures. Their significance lay in the fact that they made it less likely that the constitutional rights of a witness would be lost through entrapment or confusion.

It has been long and firmly established that the sole purpose of the immunity from self-incrimination clause of the Fifth Amendment is to protect persons from compulsion to give evidence which will expose them to the danger of criminal prosecution. Significantly affecting both the power of the government to investigate subversion and the right of witnesses under the Fifth Amendment is the case of *Ullmann* v. *United States*,[42] which sustained the Immunity Act of 1954, even as applied to state prosecutions.

The act[43] provides that when a U.S. attorney believes it necessary in the public interest to secure testimony or papers of a witness in any judicial proceeding in connection with threats to national security or defense, he may, upon approval of the Attorney General, apply to the Court for an order, directing the witness to testify or produce the evidence, provided that:

no such witness shall be prosecuted or subjected to any penalty or forfeiture for an account of any transaction, matter or thing concerning

[42] 350 U.S. 422 (1956).
[43] 18 U.S.C., 68 Stat. 746; (Supp. II), Sec. 3486.

which he is compelled, after having claimed his privilege against self-incrimination, to testify or produce evidence, nor shall testimony so compelled be used as evidence in any criminal proceeding against him in any Court.

Ullmann, who had refused on Fifth Amendment grounds to testify before a grand jury concerning his alleged Communist Party membership and activities, persisted in his refusal, in response to a Court order issued under the Immunity Act, on the ground that the act was unconstitutional. On appeal to the Supreme Court, the act was upheld and his conviction for contempt was sustained. The Court, speaking through Justice Frankfurter, held that the government may trade the right to prosecute for the privilege against self-incrimination, since the immunity need only remove the fear of criminal prosecution. Thus, if the defendant is rendered safe from prosecution, he cannot claim immunity on the ground that his testimony will disgrace, embarrass, or expose him to public disapprobation. Quoting from the sixty-year old precedent of *Brown* v. *Walker*,[44] upholding a similar statute of 1893, Justice Frankfurter asserted that "the object of the constitutional immunity from self-incrimination is fully accomplished by the statutory immunity." Since this displaces the danger of criminal prosecution, the reason for the privilege, it displaces the privilege itself. "Once the reason for the privilege ceases, the privilege ceases."

Nor is the principle of *Brown* v. *Walker* altered by new disabilities, not then existent, such as expulsion from a union, loss of employment, or adverse public sentiment. Immunity need only remove the sanction that causes the fear of criminal punishment.

More significantly, the Court further held that the provision of the act rendering the petitioner immune from prosecution "in any Court" frees him from the danger of state prosecution, and that Congress has the power to grant such immunity under its power to provide for the national security as aided by the necessary and proper clause. Congress is clearly under no constitutional obligation to afford witnesses such immunity from state prosecution in order to exercise over them its power of compulsory process, but it may do so if it wishes.

[44] 161 U.S. 591 (1896).

In the spring of 1957, the Court, in a highly significant and controversial case, reaffirmed some long-established but more recently ignored limitations on the investigative process, and apparently took the first step toward another and more far-reaching limitation, based on the First and Fourteenth Amendments. In the case of *Watkins* v. *United States*,[45] a labor union officer appeared before the House Committee on Un-American Activities and testified at length and with complete candor about his earlier associations and activities with respect to the Communist Party. He refused, however, to answer questions about similar associations and activities of others with whom he had associated but who had "long since removed themselves from the Communist movement." Watkins rested his refusal to answer questions on the ground that they were not relevant to the work of the Committee and that the Committee was without authority to undertake public exposure of persons for their past activities.

The Court sustained Watkins in his refusal to answer the questions put to him by the Committee on the ground of lack of pertinency to the subject under inquiry. Both the resolution of the House establishing the Committee and the statements of the subcommittee chairman on the day of questioning were too vague and uncertain to give Watkins sufficient indication of the matter under inquiry. The resolution setting up the Committee in 1938 authorized it, among other things, to examine into "the extent, character, and objects of un-American propaganda activities in the United States," and propaganda that attacks "the principle of the form of government as guaranteed by our Constitution." How is the witness to know what the vague term *un-American* embraces? How is he to know what is "the single principle of the form of government as guaranteed by our Constitution"?

Since the contempt statute under which witnesses may be cited to the courts provides that a witness may be punished "if he willfully makes default" by failing to respond to the subpoena or if he "refuses to answer any questions pertinent to the question under inquiry,"[46] and since he must decide at the time the questions are propounded whether or not to answer, "fundamental fair-

[45] 354 U.S. 178 (1957).
[46] 2 U.S.C. Sec. 192.

ness demands that no witness be compelled to make such a determination, with so little guidance as is available in this case." It is the duty of the interrogator, when the witness protests on the ground of pertinency, to state clearly for the record the subject under inquiry at the time and how the propounded questions are pertinent.

The statement of the subcommittee chairman in this case failed to convey to the petitioner sufficient information on the pertinency of the questions to enable him to determine whether he was within his rights in refusing to answer. The fundamental defect in such vague grants of authority to investigating agents is that it insulates the House authorizing the investigation from the witnesses subjected to the sanction of compulsory process. Thus responsibility for the use of investigative power is divorced from the actual exercise of such power. The Court argued that this situation places constitutionally protected freedoms in a danger that cannot be justified under the Bill of Rights.

Although, precisely speaking, the Court confined its holding to the narrow point of lack of pertinency and consequent denial of due process, the Chief Justice went far beyond this narrow holding and, in broad and unequivocal declarations, announced principles defining limitations on the power to investigate, including those springing from the First Amendment. He reiterated the long-established principle that the power of Congress to conduct investigations is implicit in the legislative process and is so broad as to encompass "inquiries concerning the administration of existing laws as well as proposed or possible needed statutes," surveys of defects in our social or political system with a view to finding remedies therefor, and "probes into the departments of the Federal Government to expose corruption, inefficiency, or waste."

Still, Congress is not a law enforcement or trial agency. Every inquiry must be related to its legitimate function. Consequently, there is no general authority to expose the private affairs of individuals without clear justification in terms of the functions of Congress. Moreover, the Bill of Rights limits the power of investigation, as it limits the exercise of all other powers of government. For example, witnesses may not be compelled to give evidence against themselves, nor may they be subjected to unreasonable search or seizure. Most significantly, an investigation is subject to the requirements of the First Amendment. The Court emphasized that the power to investigate in the constitutionally protected areas of "speech, press, religion, or political belief and association" may not be delegated to committees by resolutions so broad that they provide no standards for the interrogators and no measure of the need for the data, which can be balanced against the competing demands of individual freedom. Thus, Congressional committees are forbidden to ask questions which violate the rights of witnesses under the First Amendment.

Although the last point may be regarded as dictum with respect to the precise holding in the Watkins case, the Court seems to have made it the basis of decision in *Sweezy* v. *New Hampshire*,[47] decided on the same day. As has been pointed out previously in connection with state loyalty programs, all six members of the majority in this case agreed that academic and political freedoms are constitutionally protected against state investigatory power through the medium of the Fourteenth Amendment. In the words of the Court, "There is no doubt that legislative investigations, whether on a federal or state level, are capable of encroaching upon the constitutional liberties of individuals."

Indeed, it was regarded by the Court as particularly important that the power of compulsory process be carefully confined when an investigation tends to encroach upon the freedoms of teaching and of political expression and association. The interest of the state in compelling Sweezy to testify concerning the content of his lecture was insufficient when weighed against "the grave harm resulting from governmental intrusion into the intellectual life of a university." On this point, the Court made the following general observation:

The essentiality of freedom in the community of American universities is almost self-evident . . . . To impose any strait jacket upon the intellectual leaders in our colleges and universities would imperil the future of our nation. . . . . Scholarship cannot flourish in an atmosphere of suspicion and distrust. Teachers and students must always

[47] 354 U.S. 234 (1957).

remain free to inquire, to study, and to evaluate, to gain new maturity and understanding; otherwise our civilization will stagnate and die.

On Sweezy's right to refuse to answer questions concerning his association with the Progressive Party, the Court observed:

Equally manifest as a fundamental principle of a democratic society is political freedom of the individual. Our form of government is built on the premise that every citizen shall have the right to engage in political expression and association. This right was enshrined in the First Amendment of the Bill of Rights . . . . [and, of course, is made operative on the states through the Fourteenth Amendment].

Notwithstanding the divisions of the Court in the Sweezy case and the narrow grounds of decision in the Watkins case, the Court seems, in the combination of these two cases, to have expressly recognized the proposition that the First Amendment limits the power of Congressional investigative committees, and that this limitation is made operative upon the states through the due process clause of the Fourteenth Amendment.

As already indicated, the Court had in the early "cold war" years declined to consider the First Amendment as a safeguard of the right of witnesses before legislative committees. Even in the later Rumely case, only by implication did it acknowledge such an application of the Amendment. Although the limits imposed upon investigative process by the First Amendment are not clearly defined in the Watkins and Sweezy cases, they are expressly recognized and applied for the first time.

In attempting to appraise the consequences of these cases, however, it must not be assumed that they place any serious handicaps in the way of proper legislative investigation. There is no reason to believe that a Congress, bent upon the investigation of any phase of Communist activity which affects the safety of the nation, will find the Watkins case any more of an obstacle than important cases of the past have been, unless the probable necessity for a more scrupulous regard for First Amendment freedoms is regarded as a handicap. Nor is New Hampshire in danger of being overrun by subversives because of Sweezy.

The Supreme Court did not maintain in the Watkins case that Congress could not compel witnesses to appear before its committees and to testify on matters relevant to the constitutional functions of that body. It did hold that the purpose of an inquiry must be clearly stated in the authorizing resolutions, that the questions asked of witnesses must be pertinent, and that Congress must not "unjustifiably encroach upon an individual's right of privacy nor abridge his liberty of speech, press, religion or assembly." The purpose of the inquiry in this case was to expose Watkins to "the violence of public reaction" because of his past beliefs without serving any public purpose. Congress may not grant to any committee the power to expose for the sake of exposure.

It seems probable then that, in the future, resolutions authorizing investigations will have to be drawn with more particularity or that committee chairmen will have to state for the record the subject under inquiry at the time of the questioning and the manner in which the questions are pertinent thereto.

The "Cold War" and Internal Security: II

FEDERAL LEGISLATIVE CONTROL OF SUBVERSION

Modification of Clear and Present Danger Test

To the threats to basic civil liberties thus far considered in connection with the "cold war," the Court has, with few exceptions, given a negative response. That is to say, it has sustained, in one way or another, most of the legislation and executive action that has come before it. On the whole, it can be convincingly argued that the course of judicial abstention followed by the Court with respect to executive loyalty-security programs and to legislative probing into the beliefs and actions of alleged Communists is legally justified. Generally, matters relating to the appointment and removal of public officials and employees are not within the province of the courts, nor is the function of legislative investigation subject to drastic judicial control by any constitutional doctrines which have evolved since the 1880's.

Since about 1946, the tendency toward judicial self-restraint has been no less pronounced with respect to substantive legislation aimed at the control of subversives. This brings us to the three most significant cases arising from the efforts of Congress to combat the Communist threat known as the "cold war." The first concerned the non-Communist affidavit provisions of the Taft-Hartley (Labor-Management) Act of 1947, and the second and third centered on the antisedition provisions of the Alien Registration (Smith) Act of 1940. Perhaps in no previous civil liberties case had the issue of liberty versus authority been drawn more sharply, nor had the problem of balancing the interests of free speech and assembly against the interest of national security presented such complexities and difficulties. The postwar judicial trend away from application of the clear and present danger test and the preferred status of First Amendment freedoms all but reached a climax of repudiation in these cases. While giving lip service to clear and present danger, the Court in effect reverted to the dangerous tendency test of the Gitlow case.

In *American Communications Association* v. *Douds*,[1] the Court sustained Section 9(*h*) of the Taft-Hartley Act which provides that no labor union shall have access to the privileges of the National Labor Relations Act or to the facilities of the National Labor Relations Board unless each of its officers files an affidavit with the Board swearing: (1) "that he is not a member of the Communist Party or affiliated with such party," and (2) "that he does not believe in, and is not a member of or supports any organization that believes in or teaches the overthrow of the United States Government by force or by any illegal or unconstitutional methods." Chief Justice Vinson said, at the outset of his opinion, that the purpose of Congress in setting up the oath requirement was to eliminate the political strike as an obstruction to interstate commerce. On this ground the provisions of the statute were sustained against the contention that they violated freedom of speech and political opinion.

Although he avowedly accepts the conception of clear and present danger, as formulated by Holmes and Brandeis, and admits that this is also a free speech case, the Chief Justice evades the whole question of clear and present danger by the hazy argument that the statute was directed at conduct rather than speech. Said he:

Speech may be fought with speech. . . . Falsehoods and fallacies must be exposed, not suppressed, unless there is not sufficient time to avert the evil consequences of noxious doctrine by argument and education. That is the command of the First Amendment. But force may and must be met with force. Section 9(*h*) is designed to protect the public not against what Communists and others identified therein advocate or believe, but against what Congress has concluded they have done and are likely to do again.

[1] 339 U.S. 382 (1950).

With this line of argument the Chief Justice proceeded to reduce the clear and present danger doctrine to a device for the judicial balancing of interests between First Amendment freedoms, on the one hand, and the public order, on the other. Of course, the evil threatened by free speech must be serious and substantial, but this does not mean an absolutist test in terms of danger to the nation. Indeed, Vinson continued, "When the effect of a statute or ordinance upon the exercise of First Amendment freedoms is relatively small and the public interest to be protected is substantial, it is obvious that a rigid test requiring a showing of imminent danger to the security of the Nation is an absurdity."

In effecting this balancing process in the instant case, the preferred status formula of earlier cases necessarily gave way to deference to legislative judgment. The problem here was simply that of balancing what was considered to be the relatively small effects of the statute upon those freedoms, against the judgment of Congress that political strikes were evils of conduct causing substantial harm to interstate commerce. This, argued the Court, was a matter with which Congress, not the courts, was primarily concerned, and there was ample justification for the decision of Congress in this case.

The provision of the statute concerning belief in the overthrow of the government by force was construed to relate not to the ultimate overthrow of the government as a vision of the future, but to belief in the "objective overthrow" of the government as it now exists under the Constitution, by force or other illegal means. Interpreted thus, the belief provision of the oath was held to present a problem no different from that involved in the provision relating to membership in the Communist Party. It was vigorously denied that thought control was involved or that beliefs were in any way to be punished, since the only result of the statute was the possible loss of one's position as a labor leader. This, interestingly enough, was not regarded as punishment.

In the principal opinion, Chief Justice Vinson spoke only for Justices Reed and Burton. Justices Douglas, Minton, and Clark did not participate in the decision. Justices Frankfurter and Jackson concurred with the majority on the first part of the oath law, relating to membership in the Communist Party, but dissented from the portion of the opinion that upheld provisions concerning belief in the overthrow of the government by force. Justice Black dissented from the entire opinion on the ground that Section 9 (*h*) was completely invalid. Thus, the six participating justices divided 5 to 1 in sustaining the first part of the section and 3 to 3 in sustaining the second part. In his dissent, Justice Frankfurter declared that Congress had here "cast its net too indiscriminately" and had opened "the door too wide to mere speculation or uncertainty." Every rational indulgence should be made in favor of the constitutionality of a Congressional enactment, but it is not within the authority of Congress to probe into opinions which indicate no certain relationship to the Communist Party and the dangers which the statute as a whole sought to avert. Justice Jackson vigorously denounced the thought control provision, because Congress in his view has no power

to proscribe any opinion or belief which has not manifested itself in any overt act. . . . Only in the darkest periods of human history has any Western government concerned itself with mere belief . . . when it has not matured into overt action; and if that practice survives anywhere, it is in the Communist countries whose philosophies we loathe.

Rejecting the assumption that the power to forbid acts includes the power to forbid their contemplation, he asked rhetorically, "Can we say that men of our time must not even think about the propositions on which our own Revolution was justified? Or, may they think, provided they reach only one conclusion—and that the opposite of Mr. Jefferson's?" Thus Jackson asserted the unrestricted constitutional right of each member of our society to think as he will. "Thought control is a copyright of totalitarianism, and we have no claim to it."

The new interpretation of the clear and present danger rule in the Douds case and the Court's disposition of the preferred status principle easily paved the way for the decision a year later in the famous Dennis case.[2] It was this case which offered the Supreme Court its first opportunity to pass upon the validity of the Smith Act, Secs. 2 and 3 of which forbid the willful advising, teaching, or advocacy of the overthrow of any government in the United States

[2] *Dennis* v. *United States,* 341 U.S. 494 (1951).

by force or violence, and conspiring to do so. In 1948, eleven top leaders of the Communist Party of the United States were indicted under the act for willfully and knowingly conspiring to teach and advocate the overthrow of the government by force and violence, and for conspiring to organize the Communist Party for such purpose. The trial, which ran for more than eight months before District Judge Medina in New York, resulted in conviction. In his charge to the jury, Judge Medina stated that:

> it is not the abstract doctrine of overwhelming or destroying organized government by lawful means which is denounced by this law, but the teaching and advocacy of action for the accomplishment of that purpose, by language reasonably and ordinarily calculated to incite persons to such action . . . as speedily as circumstances would permit.

He stated further that the duty of the jury was confined to determining whether the evidence showed a violation of the statute, as he had interpreted it, and that the question of whether there was a clear and present danger of an evil, which Congress might prevent without violating the First Amendment, was a matter of law with which the jury had no concern. Both the charge to the jury and the conviction were upheld by the Court of Appeals in an opinion by Judge Learned Hand.

In granting certiorari, the Supreme Court limited the scope of its review to the constitutional questions of free speech under the First Amendment and due process under the Fifth Amendment. It did not review the sufficiency of evidence for supporting the jury's verdict or certain allegations relating to the conduct of the trial.

The judgment of the Court sustaining the convictions, against free speech and free assembly objections, was supported by three different opinions representing three interpretations of the clear and present danger test, not to mention a fourth by dissenters Black and Douglas.

Chief Justice Vinson, announcing the judgment of the Court and speaking also for Justices Reed, Burton, and Minton, stressed the substantial character of the government's interest in preventing its own destruction by force. This, he said, "is certainly a substantial enough interest for the Government to limit speech." Indeed, this is the ultimate value of any society, for if it is unable to protect itself from armed internal attack, it is certain that no subordinate value can be protected. The Chief Justice spoke here as though the defendants had been indicted for an overt act of attempting to overthrow the government by force, which was not the charge. They had been accused of conspiring to teach and advocate and to form a party to teach and advocate overthrow of the government by force and violence.

Considering the meaning of the phrase *clear and present danger* in such circumstances, the Chief Justice declared that it "obviously cannot mean that before the Government may act it must wait until the *putsch* is about to be executed, the plans have been laid and the signal is awaited." Vinson paid warm tribute to the Holmes-Brandeis version of clear and present danger and purported to apply it, but in reality he had adopted in its place a very different test, suggested by Judge Learned Hand in his Court of Appeals opinion. "In each case," said Judge Hand, "Courts must ask whether the gravity of the 'evil,' discounted by its improbability, justifies such invasion of free speech as is necessary to avoid the danger." Accepting this test, the Chief Justice argued that Holmes and Brandeis were not confronted with a situation comparable to that of this case, namely, a highly organized conspiracy of rigidly disciplined members "dedicated to the overthrow of the government" in the context of recurring world crises. Under the Hand formula, the danger need not be imminent. It was not important, then, that no attempt had been made here to overthrow the government. It was enough that the defendants were ready and willing to make the attempt "as soon as circumstances will permit." If, then, the evil legislated against is serious enough, advocacy may be punished, even though there is no clear and present danger of success. Put another way, the gravity of the evil decreases the necessity for its clarity and imminence. In this opinion, then, Chief Justice Vinson substituted the Hand test of *grave* and *probable* for the Holmes-Brandeis test of *clear and present danger*. He thus divested the traditional test of the vital element of *imminence* and seriously blurred the element of *clarity*. Vinson's attempt to square the Hand formula with the Holmes-Brandeis version of clear and present danger is something less than impressive. It is essentially the bad tendency test in a different garb.

Yet, as if to save something of the clear and present danger test, Vinson brings up the question of conspiracy, which he had not hitherto stressed. Rejecting the argument that a conspiracy to advocate, as distinguished from advocacy itself, cannot be constitutionally restrained since it comprises only preparation, the Chief Justice asserts: "It is the existence of the conspiracy which creates the danger," and, after all, clear and present danger "is a judicial rule to be applied as a matter of law by the courts."

In his concurring opinion, Justice Frankfurter reiterated his well-known antagonism to the clear and present danger doctrine which, through recent decisions, he thought, had become nothing more than "a sonorous formula which is in fact only a euphemistic disguise for an unresolved conflict," an inflexible dogma supporting "uncritical libertarian generalities."

Justice Jackson, who had earlier been a vigorous and eloquent defender of the clear and present danger doctrine, set forth an entirely new notion of the formula in his concurring opinion. Cases like this one, he said, require the Court "to reappraise, in the light of our own times and conditions, constitutional doctrines devised under other circumstances to stake a balance between authority and liberty." The clear and present danger test, as originally enunciated by Mr. Justice Holmes and later refined by him and Mr. Justice Brandeis, was used as a rule of evidence in particular cases involving relatively simple issues, such as the "criminality of a hot headed speech on a street corner, or circulation of a few incendiary pamphlets, or parading by some zealots behind a red flag. . . ." This was before the era of World War II had revealed "the subtlety and efficacy of modernized revolutionary techniques used by totalitarian parties." In these earlier and simpler situations it was not beyond the capacity of courts to comprehend and weigh the evidence "for decision whether there is a clear and present danger of substantive evil or a harmless letting off of steam." In such cases the danger, if there ever was a danger, has already matured by the time of the trial and does not involve prophecy. Thus Jackson would save the clear and present danger test for the relatively trivial situations involving speech and publication by individuals. But he bluntly rejected the applicability of the test to a nation-wide, organized conspiracy, such as that of the Communist Party.

In this connection he emphasized, as did none of his colleagues, that this was a conspiracy case. He accurately pointed out that what the Court was really reviewing here "is a conviction of conspiracy, after a trial for conspiracy on an indictment charging conspiracy, brought under a statute outlawing conspiracy." He noted further that the Constitution does not make conspiracy a civil right and the Court ought not to make it one now. The essence of the concept of conspiracy is that it may be an evil in itself, independent of any evil it hopes to accomplish. Conspiracy is the plotting of an unlawful act, and the execution of the act is not a part of the conspiracy unless required by statute. Thus, if Congress makes conspiracy a crime without the requirement of an overt act to establish it, as it did in the Smith Act, it is ridiculous, Jackson argued, to hold that it can punish the former only if there is a clear and present danger of the latter. Furthermore, it makes no difference that speech was used in the course of this conspiracy, for "communication is the essence of every conspiracy."

Jackson's theory seems to hold serious hazards for persons speaking or writing in concert with others, or for speech in combination with assembly, and much speaking and writing fall within these classes. Justice Jackson recognized this danger in the frank admission that he considered criminal conspiracy "a dragnet device capable of perversion into an instrument of injustice in the hands of a partisan or complacent judiciary," but it has an established place in our law and ought to be available for application against plots to undermine the whole government.

It is significant that Frankfurter and Jackson, whose votes were necessary to the majority position in this case, both expressed doubt as to the wisdom and effectiveness of the Smith Act as a method of combating communism. Although Jackson thought the Court could not hold the act unconstitutional, he took the pains to add: "I have little faith in the long-range effectiveness of this conviction to stop the rise of the Communist movement. Communism will not go to jail with those Communists."

Justice Frankfurter likewise warned that his holding of constitutionality in no way implied that he favored "the implications that lie beneath the legal issues." He rather thought that legislation of this kind tends to become "a formidable enemy of the free spirit."

There seemed to be little doubt, however, that the Court, in affirming these convictions, had narrowed the scope of protection of freedom of speech and assembly under the First Amendment. It so interpreted the clear and present danger test as to leave Congress largely free from the restrictions of the First Amendment in meeting the Communist problem. If the effect of this were confined to Communist Party cases, there would be nothing to deplore but it would be naïve to anticipate such a happy result. The contrary was forcefully put by Mr. Justice Frankfurter in his concurring opinion, just considered. Said he:

> Suppressing advocates of overthrow inevitably will also silence critics who do not advocate overthrow but fear that their criticism may be so construed. No matter how clear we may be that the defendants now before us are preparing to overthrow our Government at the propitious moment, it is self delusion to think that we can punish them for their advocacy without adding to the risks run by loyal citizens who honestly believe in some of the reforms these defendants advance. It is a sobering fact that in sustaining the conviction before us we can hardly escape restrictions on the interchange of ideas.

Yates Case Limits Effect of Dennis

The Department of Justice, not without reason, seems to have interpreted the Dennis decision as holding that the Communist Party is a criminal conspiracy, dedicated to the overthrow of the government of the United States by force and violence, and that its leaders and members may therefore be constitutionally punished. Since the Dennis decision, nearly one hundred convictions and many more indictments have been obtained for violation of the Smith Act.[3]

But in the Yates case[4] of June, 1957, the Supreme Court demonstrated that the government had taken too expansive a view of its powers under the Smith Act to prosecute Communists. The fourteen Communist leaders in the case were convicted after a

---

[3] Robert E. Cushman, *Leading Constitutional Decisions,* 11th ed. (New York, Appleton-Century-Crofts, 1958), p. 459.

[4] *Yates* v. *United States,* 354 U.S. 298.

jury trial in the District Court for the Southern District of California, on a single-count indictment charging them with conspiracy (1) to advocate and teach the duty and necessity of overthrowing the government by force and violence, and (2) to organize the Communist Party for such advocating and teaching, both with the intention of causing the overthrow of the government by force and violence as speedily as circumstances would permit doing so.

In Yates, the Court was faced, among other things, with the question whether the Smith Act forbids advocacy and teaching of forcible overthrow as an abstract principle, divorced from any effort to incite action to that end, provided that such advocacy and teaching are done with evil intent. The Court held that it does not. Since the government had relied upon the Dennis case in presenting its case against the petitioners in Yates, the Court declared that its reliance on Dennis showed a misinterpretation of that case. Indeed, it would appear that the Court in the later case was interpreting the Dennis opinion as much as it was the Smith Act.

The Court found the District Judge's charge to the jury defective, because it did not state clearly that advocacy of violent overthrow, to escape the restrictions of the First Amendment, must involve an urging to action presently or in the future. The charge to the jury in the Dennis case had met this test, argued the Court. The important and essential distinction here is that those to whom advocacy is directed must be urged to action now or in the future, and not merely to belief in something.

Dennis was concerned with a conspiracy to advocate presently the forcible overthrow of the government in the future. Action, not advocacy, was to be postponed "until circumstances would permit."

The Court emphasized that Dennis still stands, and that its reasoning, properly viewed against the facts of the case, is not in conflict with the opinion in Yates.

Yet the Yates opinion seems to represent a departure from the belief, expressed by a majority of the justices in Dennis, that the secret nature of the Communist Party and its indoctrination activities make any distinction between advocacy of action and advocacy of belief somewhat thin, when the defendants are members of such a tightly disciplined organization as the Communist Party. Moreover, the Dennis case seems clearly to indicate that when a conspiracy itself is a clear and present danger, little evidence is required to show that the nature of the advocacy by the conspirators presents a clear and present danger.

On its face, the Smith Act does not indicate the distinction here made by the Court, but it is argued that the history of the act shows it was aimed at the advocacy and teaching of concrete action for the forcible overthrow of the government, and not of principles divorced from action. Moreover, since the word *advocate* in the free speech area has traditionally meant advocacy of action,[5] Congress must have intended such a meaning in the act. "In construing the Act," the Court declared, "we should not assume that Congress chose to disregard a constitutional danger zone so clearly marked" as the free speech guarantees of the First Amendment. Thus the Court construes the Smith Act as forbidding the only kind of advocacy it could constitutionally forbid, namely, that which amounts to actual incitement to action directed to the forcible overthrow of the government. It seems then that the Court, without using the famous phrase, has swung back in the direction of the Brandeis-Holmes conception of the clear and present danger test.

Were Congress to amend the Smith Act to forbid, in precise terms, advocacy of forcible overthrow of the government with the intent to bring about such an end, would the Court hold the act unconstitutional? On the basis of its opinion in Yates, and the interpretation there given of the Dennis opinion, it would logically so hold. Still, it would be hazardous to predict that logic would prevail in these circumstances, for the pull of judicial self-restraint has in the past been at its maximum when the Court was dealing with the validity of acts of Congress relating to national security.

It would also seem, in the light of Yates, that punishment of simple membership in the Communist Party would involve an unconstitutional application of the Smith Act, but this question

---

[5] Citing *Fox* v. *Washington*, 236 U.S. 273, *Schenck* v. *United States*, 249 U.S. 47, and *Gitlow* v. *New York*, 268 U.S. 652.

has not been precisely determined by the Supreme Court as yet.[6]

It may be doubted that important practical results will flow from the distinction between advocacy of abstract doctrine with evil intent and advocacy of action at some indefinite time in the future, so far as jury findings are concerned. The Court clearly indicated that the instructions given in Dennis would have been adequate in Yates. This, on a retrial, would seem to eliminate the difficulty.

Although it was generally thought that the Douds and Dennis cases had divested the clear and present danger test of its vitality in the field of federal legislation, the Yates case seems to mark at least a partial reversion to the Brandeis-Holmes version of the famous doctrine, albeit by implication. As reinterpreted in the Dennis case, the clear and present danger rule did not require evidence that the Communist Party posed a real and imminent danger of fomenting a violent revolution in the United States, but only that it intended to do so when and if circumstances permitted. Under the Yates rule of interpretation, the government will no longer be able to convict and punish members of the Communist Party for expressing a mere belief in the violent overthrow of the government. It will have to prove that the defendants actually intended to overthrow the government, or to persuade others to do so by language calculated to incite action to that end either immediately or in the future. Thus the danger must be clear, if not imminent.

Federal Sedition Statutes Supersede State Sedition Laws

Again, in 1956, the Court adopted the device of statutory construction to limit the applicability of state sedition laws. In *Pennsylvania* v. *Nelson*,[7] Chief Justice Warren, speaking for the Court, found Pennsylvania's antisubversive legislation, to the extent that it punished subversion against the United States, to be unconstitutional for the following reasons: (1) the scheme of federal regulation is so persuasive as to make reasonable the inference that Congress left no room for the states to supplement it; (2) the

[6] *Lightfoot* v. *United States,* 353 U.S. 979 (1957), and 355 U.S. 2 (1957).
[7] 350 U.S. 497 (1956).

federal statutes touch a field in which the national interest is so dominant that the federal system must be assumed to preclude enforcement of state laws on the same subject; and (3) "Enforcement of state sedition acts presents a serious danger of conflict with the administration of the federal program." The Chief Justice was careful to point out that this decision did not affect the right of the state to enforce its sedition laws when the federal government has not occupied the field, that it did not limit the right of the state to protect itself against violence and sabotage at any time, and that it did not preclude the state from prosecution where the same act is both a state and a federal offense. Here, however, there was no evidence, in a long record, of sedition against the government of Pennsylvania.

Although the Court had in this case stated that the pre-emption issue turned upon the Smith Act alone, it supported its decision by relying not on the Smith Act alone, but also on the Internal Security Act of 1950 and the Communist Control Act of 1954, which together constituted a comprehensive system of Communist control. In determining the pre-emptive effect to be given this scheme of legislation, the Court relied on criteria developed in commerce clause cases.[8] Under the doctrine of national supremacy, it would seem clear that Congress has the power to bar state prosecution in the interest of national security. In the Ullmann case, previously discussed, the Court had found that a federal immunity statute precluded state criminal prosecution on this ground.

SUMMARY ANALYSIS OF CHAPTERS 6 AND 7

The generally strong libertarian spirit which characterized the opinions of the Court during the decade after 1937 rapidly subsided with the onset of the "cold war," except with respect to Negro rights and certain procedural guarantees. This change in judicial attitude then coincided with what was apparently a marked change in public opinion with respect to the seriousness and scope of the Communist threat.

[8] See, for example, *Rice* v. *Sante Fe Elevator Corp.*, 331 U.S. 218, 219–230 (1947).

Response of the Court to "Cold War" Programs

The loyalty cases, whether on national or state level, have shown the Court reluctant to interpose any obstacles to the power of the government to erect bars against the employment, or to effect dismissal, of persons with unsatisfactory affiliations. In no case, until Sweezy, was the substantive power of government to act in such matters questioned. On the national level the Court has condemned the listing of organizations by the Attorney General as subversive without a hearing, has limited the authority of the Loyalty Review Board to review cases on its own motion, and has denied the applicability of summary suspension and dismissal procedures to employees in nonsensitive positions. At the state level it has finally condemned state loyalty statutes, embodying the doctrine of guilt by association by making mere membership in a subversive organization a conclusive presumption of disloyalty. The Court has also held that no state employee may be automatically dismissed, without charges, notice, hearing, or the right of appeal, merely because he invokes the privilege against self-incrimination in a federal investigation. More significantly, freedom of expression and association of state employees seems to be protected against the state investigatory power unless the state can show that an overriding public interest is threatened.

With subversive control programs relating to aliens or unnaturalized citizens, likewise, the Court has hesitated to intervene in behalf of basic freedoms. The complete power of Congress over the admission of aliens to the country and the equally complete responsibility of the Executive for the conduct of foreign affairs support this passive attitude on the part of the Court. But in matters relating to aliens, the attitude of judicial restraint has been much more pronounced in later cases than in those decided during the World War II period. Past membership in the Communist Party without knowledge of the Party's advocacy may now be made the basis for deportation of an alien, because "under our constitutional system the determination of policies for the deportation of aliens is the exclusive concern of Congress." [9]

A similar change in judicial attitude has been noted in connec-

[9] *Galvan v. Press,* 347 U.S. 522 (1954).

tion with cases involving denaturalization of naturalized citizens. In the World War II cases, the Court required the government to support its charge of fraudulent and illegal naturalization by "evidence that is clear, unequivocal and convincing." But in 1949 the Court ruled that the strict procedural standards of a criminal trial need not be observed in denaturalization cases.[10]

In a virtually undeviating line of precedent, extending over three quarters of a century, the courts had exercised little restraint upon the alleged violation of the rights of individuals and groups arising from legislative investigations. Especially from McGrain, in 1927, to 1955 the Court had insisted that it was unable to find illegal abuses of the investigatory power "unless it was obvious that there was a usurpation of functions exclusively vested in the executive, or in the Courts." In a series of cases from 1955 on, however, the Court has marked more clearly the boundaries of legislative investigation. The following limitations on the power of investigating committees seem to have been established in some cases firmly, in others perhaps tentatively.

The investigation must be clearly in aid of a valid legislative function. The questions asked of witnesses must be pertinent to the subject of the inquiry. The valid purpose of the inquiry must be clearly stated in the authorizing resolution. Witnesses may not be compelled to give evidence against themselves, unless they are protected from the danger of criminal prosecution by an immunity statute; nor may a witness be subjected to unreasonable search and seizure. True, the privilege against self-incrimination must be claimed by the witness, but no special formula of words is required so long as his intention is made reasonably clear. Moreover, criminal intent on the part of the witness must be shown by a clear disposition of his objection to questions, before he can be cited for contempt. There can be no investigation into the private affairs of a person for the sole purpose of exposure. Most significantly, it appears that both Congressional and state legislative investigating committees are forbidden to ask questions that violate the rights of witnesses to freedom of expression and association under the First and Fourteenth Amendments.

[10] *Klaprott* v. *United States,* 335 U.S. 601 (1949). But see p. 136.

Antisedition Legislation and the Modification
of "Clear and Present Danger"

The tendency toward judicial self-restraint during the early "cold war" years was equally marked with respect to substantive legislation aimed at the control of subversion. In the Douds case the Court abandoned the preferred position principle in favor of deference to legislative judgment, in the question of the anti-Communist oath provisions of the Taft-Hartley Act. Only Douglas and Black still pleaded for the preferred status of First Amendment freedoms.

Then, in the famous Dennis case, the substantial majority of the Court seemed to go all the way in rejecting the Holmes-Brandeis version of the clear and present danger, in favor of the old reasonable tendency test, although it was clothed in the garb of a new clear and present danger test. Whereas under the Holmes-Brandeis theory, immediate danger to a substantial interest was necessary to justify invasion of free speech, Vinson argued in Dennis that if the interest be substantial, the danger need not be imminent. It was not important in this case that the defendants had made no effort to overthrow the government; it was sufficient that they were willing to make the attempt when circumstances permitted. The intention to bring about the overthrow of the government by violence at an indefinite time in the future, when combined with conspiracy to advocate such overthrow, presented a sufficient danger to justify punishment without the necessity of proving any immediate danger from advocacy. In a word, the Court substituted for the clear and present danger doctrine the grave and probable test of Judge Learned Hand.

There seemed little doubt at the time that this reinterpretation of constitutional doctrine had narrowed the scope of protection of freedom of speech and assembly; that the clear and present danger test had been divested of its substance so far as Congressional legislation was concerned, and that Congress had been given a free hand on legislation against subversion.

It now appears that these conclusions may have been premature, for the Court in its interpretation of the pertinent provisions of the Smith Act in the Yates case, in 1957, seemed, by implication at least, to revert to the Holmes-Brandeis concept of clear and present danger. Whether or not this is true may not be of paramount significance, for clear and present danger is not the only formula by which First Amendment freedoms may be sustained, although by results it has been the most effective one. It will be remembered that the Court began its protection of freedom of expression from state restraint under the leadership of Chief Justice Hughes, in 1931, with no reference to clear and present danger. The unembellished application of due process was enough.

Be this as it may, the most important aspect of the Court's work in the area of civil liberties since 1955 has been a line of cases upholding the rights of individuals against measures designed to repress communism. It should be noted, however, that the Court, in reverting to its former libertarian position after 1955, did not face up to the important constitutional issues raised in the litigation. Instead, it resorted to the control of procedure and statutory construction. The record of the Court during these years points up especially the effectiveness of statutory construction in limiting certain aspects of the antisubversion programs. By this device the Court can limit inroads upon the freedom of the individual without settling constitutional issues pertinent to possible dangers of the future.

It would be easy to say that these changes in the attitude of the Court toward the problem of individual freedom versus internal security are simply a response to the climate of opinion in which the Court operates. This, however, cannot be demonstrated, for no one knows whether the justices follow the dominant view of the nation or share it, assuming that it is known. It may be that the Court concluded, along with many other citizens, that individual liberty had been unduly restricted under the security programs. Such a view found editorial expression in the *New York Times,* of June 24, 1957, in these words: ". . . we think no objective observer could deny that during the past decade a drastic imbalance occurred in which individual liberty grievously suffered in the hopeless quest for an absolute security."

However, it should not be surprising if, in times like the period since 1947-49, justices are responsive to the dominant trends of thought and emotion of the society in which they live and work.

This is made easier by the fact that the Supreme Court, whether by accident or by design, has so fashioned its precedents as to allow itself very wide discretion in interpreting or rejecting a statute. But in all of this, one thing seems reasonably certain: When the nation faces a crisis seriously threatening its safety, all formulas are likely to fall before the one overriding formula, that constitutional liberties may be infringed in the government's enforcement of its prior right to survive.

8

Summary of Achievements and Continuing Threats

There can be little question that the preservation of civil liberty is one of the paramount issues facing the American people today. The problem, in its broadest and most elemental sense, is the age-old one of establishing a satisfactory balance between liberty and authority. In a special way, this has been the persistent problem of constitutional democracy, and it has become vastly more difficult to preserve the freedom of the individual in a society such as that of the United States, which demands so great a measure of power and complex organization in order to insure its efficiency and security. The object of the preceding pages has been to assay the record of the Supreme Court of the United States in safeguarding individual freedom in the significant years since 1937. The purpose of this chapter is merely to summarize some of the judicial achievements of this period and to call attention to some continuing threats to basic liberties.

JUDICIAL ACHIEVEMENTS

The outstanding judicial achievements stem from the application of the principle, first enunciated in 1925, that the *due process* of law clause of the Fourteenth Amendment extends the basic guarantees of the First Amendment into the areas of state and local government. The major part of the progress made by this nation in the field of civil liberties is the product of judicial decisions from 1925 on. It was in this period that a conscious and deliberate attempt was made in Supreme Court decisions to pour practical meaning into specific provisions of the Bill of Rights and the Fourteenth Amendment, such as freedom of speech, press and assembly, freedom of religion, due process of law, and equal protection of the laws.

166

Coupled with this significant development was the application, and largely the formulation, of the new doctrines of "clear and present danger" and "preferred status" of First Amendment freedoms. Despite the diversity of judicial opinion with respect to these doctrines, and the fact that they now appear to have been, at least temporarily, abandoned, the record of the Court in sustaining civil liberties claims in this period is written largely in the application of these doctrines.

Their application to a variety of new situations has been considered in Chapter 3. It has been established that indiscriminate curbing of peaceful picketing, whether by statute or by injunction, is a denial of free speech in violation of the due process clause of the Fourteenth Amendment. Peaceful picketing may be restrained, however, when conducted in a context of violence or when designed to thwart a validly declared state policy.

The general right of the press and of individuals to comment on and criticize pending judicial proceedings, as well as past judicial acts, seems well established. Such comment is punishable only where there is danger of interference with the fair administration of justice.

The orderly distribution of handbills, leaflets, and books on streets and in other public places, and the sale of noncommercial literature in such public places, without prior official permission or payment of a license tax, were sustained in a series of cases as the proper exercise of freedom of the press under the due process clause of the Fourteenth Amendment. Although the sound truck cases are, as previously indicated, inconclusive, it seems clear that the use of sound-amplifying devices is entitled to the protection of freedom of expression guaranteed by the Fourteenth Amendment. The volume of sound, time of broadcasting, and other conditions may, however, be regulated by narrowly drawn statutes.

Motion pictures have been brought within the free press protection of the First and Fourteenth Amendments, but here, too, further clarification is needed.

In the field of religious freedom, the Supreme Court has vastly extended the protection afforded by the free exercise provision of the First Amendment, and in some particulars it has clarified the meaning of religious freedom. It is now clear that no government may interfere in any manner with the free exercise of religion, except to preserve order and to prevent or punish crime. With respect to the delimitation and clarification of the "establishment" clause, the more recent contributions of the Court have been conspicuously less impressive. Despite the confusion and contradictions, it does seem that a fairly complete separation of church and state has been established. It is clear that all direct governmental aid to religion is forbidden by the Constitution.

It is undoubtedly in the field of race relations that judicial protection of basic freedoms has been most consistent and substantial since the late 1930's. Indeed, since 1946 the strongest affirmative influence of the Court has been in this sphere. With the repeated and emphatic outlawing of the "white primary," as well as of other methods of Negro disfranchisement, the road seems to have been paved for Negroes to go on to achieve genuine political equality in the South.

The judicial condemnation of racial discrimination in other areas has been equally impressive. An effective blow even to private racial discrimination was struck by the Court in a series of restrictive covenant cases, holding that the state courts may not enforce racially discriminatory covenants with respect to the acquisition, occupancy, and disposition of real estate. It may be added that racial segregation in the armed services has been virtually eliminated without benefit of judicial assistance.

Of course, the most far-reaching judicial achievement in the banishment of racial discrimination is reflected in the decisions condemning racial segregation in public transportation, public recreation, and public education.

There are, however, continuing threats to civil liberty, many of which go beyond the reach of judicial review, and to these we now turn.

CONTINUING THREATS

Lack of Standards of Loyalty

One of the most serious threats to civil liberty in a "cold war" period is the failure (owing to inability or unwillingness of those who undertake, or whose duty it is, to safeguard our national security) to devise clear tests or standards for discovering those who are a menace to national security and ought to be punished or restrained. They have no formula for separating the subversive and disloyal from persons with political and economic views more radical or progressive than those of the dominant element of the community. Since we have no formula for discovering subversive or disloyal persons, we must, the reasoning seems to go, restrain and punish all whom we suspect of being disloyal or subversive. In this way, fear and suspicion far too often become the test. Since there are no standards for determining what is loyalty, fear of new ideas frequently leads to equating loyalty with orthodoxy or conformity.

Such extremes have been noted in connection with the work of certain legislative investigating committees, the loyalty-security programs, and loyalty oath requirements.

It is apparent that many drastic measures of the loyalty-security administration have been taken not against subversive or disloyal persons, but against radical, or even liberal, American citizens whose conversation, reading, or association departs from what is regarded as the proper orthodox position. Especially threatening in this connection is the Attorney General's list of subversive organizations, which serves as the basis of the loyalty systems. It should be noted that investigators are directed, in determining a person's loyalty, to consider his "membership in, affiliation with, or sympathetic association with" organizations designated by the Attorney General as subversive, Communist, and so on. This list has been characterized by former Senator Harry Cain, an erstwhile Republican member of the Subversive Activities Control Board, as a "heinous thing," which frightens people away from joining anything for "fear that in terms of evolution the group could be termed antagonistic and they would lose their jobs 25 years later."[1] Mr. Cain stated in March, 1955, that he did not know the status of many of the organizations on the list and that he doubted "if anyone else does," that the Control Board had been petitioned to hear only 13 cases, and that other organizations only alleged to be subversive "may remain on the hateful roll for a hundred years."

[1] See the *Washington Post* and *Times Herald,* March 29, 1955.

Abuse of Legislative Investigation

Abuses connected with the efforts of certain House and Senate committees to discover and expose the alleged disloyalty or subversive conduct of individuals have deprived many innocent persons of their civil liberty, not to mention their jobs. These abuses also stand as a constant threat to the civil liberty of others. Some committees have inflicted punishment upon government employees and private citizens which were more severe than if they had been fined or jailed. The loss of one's position on a mere accusation of disloyalty may not be punishment in the legal sense, but if it smears a man's reputation and blasts his chosen career, for which he has spent years in preparation, it imposes punishment worse than a fine or jail sentence. As Professor Robert E. Cushman put it, to say that such a person "has not been punished for crime by a legislative, and therefore political, body is to quibble with words."[2] Referring to the same situation, Professor Zechariah Chafee remarks: "It is something quite new to punish men drastically who have done nothing wrong, merely for fear they might do something wrong. Such a practice is wholly alien to the traditions of English speaking freedom."[3] The Court seems to have administered a substantial setback to the more flagrant of these practices in the Watkins and Sweezy cases. But, as shown in the preceding chapter, the remedy lies primarily with Congress and the state legislatures, and ultimately with the voters of the country. The present climate of public opinion does not seem too encouraging for early results.

Guilt by Association

Chapter 7 noted that the loyalty-security programs and the legislative investigations of subversive activities have sometimes led to use of the doctrine of guilt by association as a test of loyalty.

The application of such a doctrine seriously imperils the ancient right and practice of voluntary association. The right of voluntary association for purposes of discussion has accounted for most of

[2] "American Civil Liberties in Mid-Twentieth Century," *The Annals,* Vol. 275 (May, 1951), p. 4.

[3] "Investigations of Radicalism and Laws Against Subversion," in Clair Wilcox, ed., *Civil Liberties Under Attack* (Philadelphia, University of Pennsylvania Press, 1951), p. 57.

our political and social progress, and it lies at the very grass roots of democracy. Many of our now well-established and unquestioned orthodoxies stem from heterodoxies propounded by small, often despised groups. An obvious example is abolition of slavery.

The possibility of forming associations for the purpose of discussing public issues and of promoting public causes is an essential part of the American tradition of freedom, and has a firm constitutional basis. Freedom of speech under the First Amendment has always meant more than the right of an isolated individual to speak and publish his ideas. From the outset it has involved the liberty of the individual to associate himself with other individuals for the advocacy of a common cause and for petitioning the government.

A serious danger of any widespread attack on nonconformity and dissent is that it may lead to the development of the kind of society in which freedom of inquiry, criticism, initiative, and originality cannot thrive—a society in which civil servants are afraid to read certain publications or to join reputable organizations; in which teachers are reluctant to discuss controversial issues in the classroom; in which loyal and well-meaning people hesitate to join organizations or to advocate reforms.[4] This would be hazardous to the American heritage at any time, but especially at a time like the present, when the nation faces some of the most baffling problems of its history—problems whose effective solution requires the best that a system of free enterprise in ideas can produce in the years ahead. For this, in turn, the nation needs, as never before, public servants and government advisers, business and professional leaders, scientists, scholars, and teachers who have the capacity and will to engage in bold, independent thinking about new and difficult problems. Unless we are free to encourage and develop these qualities in an atmosphere of freedom and good will, we may lose the very things we seek to make secure. It cannot be too often reiterated that the purpose of national security in a free society is to preserve freedom.

The error of those who would destroy liberty in the name of national security is, as Alan Barth has suggested, "that they con-

[4] See H. S. Commager, *Freedom, Loyalty, Dissent* (New York, Oxford University Press, 1954), pp. 17–32.

fuse loyalty with orthodoxy. Acting upon this confusion, they tend to suppress diversity and to insist upon a rigid conformity."[5] Such confusion may reduce loyalty to a set of enforced gestures and rituals, and this is precisely what loyalty in a free society is not. It cannot be coerced. National loyalty of free men is primarily belief in, and voluntary acceptance of, certain principles and ideals of freedom which the citizen will defend with his life, if necessary. Thus the highest loyalty of the American is to those fundamental principles of freedom, for the preservation of which this Republic was established and which necessarily make for intellectual and spiritual diversity. To say this is not, of course, to question the wisdom of adequate security measures, but such measures should be tested against the constitutionally guaranteed freedom of the individual.

Private Invasion of Civil Liberties

In addition to, and far more widespread than, governmental invasion of civil liberties, with which this book has been concerned, is the ever present danger that the civil liberties of the individual may be encroached upon by other individuals. It is mainly the states and not the federal government which can prevent this kind of abuse. It is clear from the language of the federal Bill of Rights and of the Fourteenth Amendment that neither restricts private or individual action unrelated to public action. Moreover, under the Constitution, the federal government possesses only limited powers to prevent individuals from interfering with the freedom of other individuals. An important example of such limited power is the federal protection of a qualified voter in his right to vote for members of the Congress. With few exceptions, however, the only effective safeguard against individual invasion of individual rights is a vigorous and persistent public opinion operating on state legislatures, executives, and courts.

Public Opinion: Safeguard and Threat

Although this study is concerned with the role of the Supreme Court in defending our fundamental liberties, it would be remiss not to point out that neither this nor any other court can preserve

[5] Alan Barth, *The Loyalty of Free Men* (New York, Viking, 1950), p. 3.

our liberties without the support of a strong and deliberate public opinion, favorable to civil liberty and its preservation. Professor Robert E. Cushman made a most lucid and forceful analysis of the vital relationship between civil liberty and public opinion in a lecture at Cornell University in 1944. Professor Cushman's thesis in brief, is that public opinion, in any meaningful sense for constitutional democracy, cannot exist without civil liberty, and that civil liberty cannot survive without the support of "an intelligent and vigorous public opinion which believes in civil liberty and will not tolerate its suppression." [6] He sees no reason to believe that courts will be able or willing to defend civil liberty if the people themselves abandon their share of the responsibility.

Public opinion then can be a threat to, as well as a safeguard of, civil liberty. The basis of the present threat is the unhealthy state of public opinion with respect to our basic freedoms. A considerable segment of American public opinion, some of it influential, seems to be characterized by an unreasoning fear—fear of everything except the orthodox and the known. We have seen political demagogues designedly arousing this fear for their own political profit, and others blindly and unwittingly nurturing it. It has bred a spirit of intolerance against independent and original thinking which could, if not arrested, seriously impair our strength to combat the forces of evil—Communist and others— that threaten us.

Of course, this spirit of intolerance is not entirely a current phenomenon. It has characterized public opinion in other periods of our history. It has merely assumed more virulent forms in the face of the Communist menace and the difficult problems of social adjustment confronting us. Over thirty years ago, Charles Evans Hughes, a former member of the Supreme Court and later Chief Justice of the United States, made an observation on this point that is even more sharply pertinent today. Speaking as President of the American Bar Association, he said:[7]

[6] "Civil Liberty and Public Opinion," in Carl Becker and others, *Safeguarding Civil Liberty Today* (Ithaca, Cornell University Press, 1945), p. 96.
[7] "Liberty and Law," Annual Address, President of the American Bar Association, Detroit, Mich., September 2, 1925.

The most ominous sign of our time, as it seems to me, is the indication of the growth of an intolerant spirit. It is the more dangerous when armed, as it usually is, with sincere conviction. It is a spirit whose wrath must be turned away by the soft answers of a sweet reasonableness. It can be exorcised only by invoking the Genius which watched over our infancy and has guided our development—a good Genius—still potent let us believe—the American spirit of civil and religious liberty. Our institutions were not devised to bring about uniformity of opinion; if they had been, we might well abandon hope. It is important to remember, as has well been said, that "the essential characteristic of true liberty is, that under its shelter many different types of life and character and opinion and belief can develop unmolested and unobstructed." Nowhere could this shelter be more necessary than in our own country with its different racial stocks, variety of faiths, and the manifold interests and opinions which attest the vigor and zest of our intellectual life. . . . The interests of liberty are peculiarly those of individuals, and hence of minorities, and freedom is in danger of being slain at her own altars if the passion for uniformity and control of opinion gathers head.

It has been said that the most effective censorship in a democracy is not legal censorship but public opinion. Control of the expression of thought and opinion in a dictatorship is imposed by force but, as Mr. Paul Hoffman has pointed out:[8]

. . . discussion, criticism, and debate can be stifled by fear, as well as by force. Persecution by public opinion can be as powerful as purges and pogroms. School teachers, government clerks and officials and even businessmen can be frightened out of their rights under the First Amendment as effectively as if that Amendment were repealed. Frightened men are at best irresponsible in their actions and at worst dangerous. Of all the forms of tyranny over the mind of man, none is more terrible than fear.

The irony of all this is that it has occurred in a nation that has grown to its present status of strength and greatness largely because it has encouraged nonconformity and dissent.

Worse than this spirit of intolerance born of fear is the apparent indifference of an even larger segment of American public opinion toward the value of civil liberty and what is happening to it

[8] "American Freedom and Business," in Allan Maxwell, ed., *The Present Danger* (Dallas, Southern Methodist University Press, 1953), p. 12.

today. It is worse because it furnishes the soil in which fear and intolerance are nurtured.[9]

Apparently many of us do not value our liberties enough to exercise them, and if we persist in this neglect we shall surely lose them. Passivity is especially perilous in these difficult and troubled times when thinking is undoubtedly the big job before us. But if thinking is to be fruitful, it must issue in expression. There is no reason to suppose that free institutions can long survive in a dormant state. They can be preserved only if they are made a living force.

In this connection, there naturally comes to mind our greatest preceptor of civil liberties, although he did not use the words. Mr. Jefferson, too, lived in an age when so-called foreign ideologies were greatly feared and when the government had tried to coerce opinion in the name of national security. He, too, was charged with being unpatriotic and subversive by his political enemies. But he defended the unpopular Thomas Paine whose book, *The Age of Reason,* was condemned by people who, he suspected, had not read it. He did not fear ideas with which he disagreed, believing that "error of opinion may be tolerated so long as reason" is free to combat it. Indeed, he knew, as we must know, that without willingness to tolerate error, there can be no freedom to pursue truth. Jefferson, too, lived in a dangerous age, and he knew that liberty involved risk, but he thought it more than worth the risk. It is true that he did not face the danger of the atom or hydrogen bomb, but it is no less true that the faith and courage reflected in the following passage from his first Inaugural Address will always be pertinent and essential to any system of liberty. His words were: "If there be any among us who would wish to dissolve this union or change its republican form, let them stand undisturbed as monuments of the safety with which error of opinion may be tolerated where reason is left free to combat it." The same spirit of faith and courage was echoed by a judicial champion of individual freedom a century and a quarter later, when Justice Brandeis declared:[10]

---

[9] Samuel A. Stouffer, *Communism, Conformity, and Civil Liberties* (New York, Doubleday, 1955), pp. 56, 68, 82.

[10] *Whitney v. California,* 274 U.S. 357, 377 (1927).

Those who won our independence believed that the final end of the state was to make men free to develop their faculties, and that in its government the deliberative forces should prevail over the arbitrary. They valued liberty both as an end and as a means. They believed liberty to be the secret of happiness and courage to be the secret of liberty. They believed that freedom to think as you will and to speak as you think are means indispensable to the discovery and spread of political truth; that without free speech and assembly discussion would be futile; that with them, discussion affords ordinarily adequate protection against the dissemination of noxious doctrine; that the greatest menace to freedom is an inert people; that public discussion is a political duty; and that this should be a fundamental principle of the American government. They recognized the risks to which all human institutions are subject. But they knew that order cannot be secured merely through fear of punishment for its infraction; that it is hazardous to discourage thought, hope and imagination; that repression breeds hate; that hate menaces stable government; that the path of safety lies in the opportunity to discuss freely supposed grievances and proposed remedies; and that the fitting remedy for evil counsels is good ones.

Finally, it may be said that we have found solutions to the problems of freedom in the past, and there is no valid reason why we shall not find solutions to current and future problems which do and will confront us. From the record of the past, however, it should be clear to all of us that we shall preserve our freedoms not by taking counsel of our fears and our hates, but rather by taking counsel of our faith, our courage, and our intelligence. And this we had better do, for the goal we seek is preservation of the greatest heritage of western thought and civilization—the essential integrity, dignity, and freedom of the individual personality.

Table of Cases

Index